W9-DGX-050

Outboard Engines

Outboard Engines

Maintenance, Troubleshooting, and Repair

Edwin R. Sherman

International Marine
Camden, Maine

To my father, Edwin C. Sherman, who began
teaching me about things mechanical and electrical before
he taught me to ride a bicycle.

International Marine/
Ragged Mountain Press

A Division of The McGraw·Hill Companies

10   9   8   7   6

Library of Congress Cataloging-in-Publication Data
Sherman, Edwin R.
    Outboard Engines : maintenance, troubleshoot-
ing, and repair / Edwin R. Sherman.
        p.   cm.
    Includes index.
    ISBN 0-07-057856-7
    1. Outboard motors—Maintenance and repair—
Handbooks, manuals, etc.   I. Title.
VM771.S54 1997
623.8'7234'0288—dc20   96-6562
                                                     CIP

Questions regarding the content of this book should
be addressed to:

International Marine
P.O. Box 220
Camden, ME 04843

Questions regarding the ordering of this book should
be addressed to:

The McGraw-Hill Companies
Customer Service Department
P.O. Box 547
Blacklick, OH 43004
Retail customers: 1-800-262-4729
Bookstores: 1-800-722-4726

Outboard Engines is printed on acid-free paper

Outboard Engines is typeset in Adobe Times.

Edited by John Kettlewell, John Vigor, Tom McCarthy

Technical review by Lincoln Davis III

Production by Publishers' Design and Production
Services, Inc.

Printed by Quebecor, Fairfield, PA

Illustrated by Geoffrey N. Skog

Photographs by Susan Thorpe Waterman

Cover design by Tim Seymour

Cover photo: Mercury's 200-h.p. DFI, courtesy Mercury Marine.

Contents

Preface

This book was written to help you maintain and repair your outboard engine, and to diagnose running problems. It won't turn you into an expert mechanic, but it will give you the confidence to carry out routine maintenance, diagnostic tests, and minor repairs.

I must point out that this book is not a substitute for the factory workshop manual covering your particular engine. You'll still need to consult your workshop manual, and when this is most important, I'll point it out.

Then why would you need this book, if you have to consult a workshop manual anyway? Well, the problem with workshop manuals is that they mostly don't help you to diagnose problems. They are textbooks for mechanics who have done the diagnosis and are about to attack the problem. This book tells you how to diagnose.

The other thing about workshop manuals is that they can't know where you would like to start or stop. They can be quite intimidating unless somebody shows you how to use them. For example, you may want to have a look at your water-pump impeller, but in the workshop manual that may be just part of a long process of dismantling the entire lower unit. Where do you enter and exit the workshop manual? This book tells you.

As a matter of fact, the idea for this book was born as I watched people trying to do their own work, often with frustrated looks in their eyes, flipping wildly through pages of manuals, not even knowing which section of the manual to begin with. This book will take care of that problem.

There will, of course, always be certain jobs that you simply can't do yourself, jobs that you will have to turn over to a professional, factory-trained mechanic because the repairs call for specialized tools, a high degree of expertise, or both. But at least when you do turn your engine over, you'll feel confident that you are an informed consumer. You'll be better able to describe your engine's problem to the mechanic, and by doing the diagnostic work yourself you won't be paying him to do it at hourly rates of twice what you're earning.

I suggest you read right through this book straight away to get a feel of what it's all about. Skip and skim, if you like, but plow through it and see what it contains. Then, when you need more specific information you'll know where to find it.

With the help of *Outboard Engines,* you'll feel comfortable about performing your own outboard maintenance. You'll be perfectly capable of handling all minor service and repair problems. And, by following the procedures outlined here, you should be able to diagnose minor problems before they become big ones. In short, if you follow my guidelines, your engine should give you many years of boating pleasure and troublefree service.

Good luck, and happy boating!

Ed Sherman

Chapter 1

The Basics: What Makes Your Engine Tick

Before you can fix a sick engine, you have to know what makes a healthy engine run. The principle is pretty simple: A piston fits into each cylinder. When fuel explodes on top of the piston, the piston is forced to move in the only direction it can, down the cylinder. The piston, which is connected by a rod to a crankshaft, turns this downward motion into something more useful by rotating the crankshaft. The crankshaft, in turn, shoves the piston back up the cylinder for more action.

Your Engine's Four Basic Needs

All outboard engines must:

- Admit a mixture of fuel and air.
- Compress that mixture.
- Ignite the compressed mixture.
- Clear away the burned gases.

Remember those four needs: fuel, compression, ignition, and exhaust. They'll come in handy when you're troubleshooting. And they're valid for all kinds of internal combustion engines, two-strokes and four-strokes; gasoline engines and diesels.

Two-stroke engines complete the full cycle of fuel induction, compression, ignition, and exhaust with just two strokes of the piston in the cylinder, one up and one down.

In four-stroke engines, the piston must travel up twice and down twice—four strokes in all—to complete the same cycle. The pay-off is that four-strokes are more efficient than two-strokes. Later, we'll discuss in more depth the relative advantages of two-stroke and four-stroke engines. Right now, what you need to know is that two-strokes are more powerful for their weight, so you get a lot of horsepower from a light engine. They're also mechanically simpler. But they are gas guzzlers and don't particularly like slow running. Their greatest sin is that they burn their lubricating oil along with the gasoline. This causes so much exhaust pollution that the U.S. Environmental Protection Agency (EPA) is forcing two-stroke outboard-engine manufacturers to reduce hydrocarbon emissions by 75 percent within the next 10 years. (You'll find more information about that in Chapter 11.)

Four-stroke engines are heavier, and usually costlier, because they need fuel-intake valves and exhaust valves. But they're more economical to run than two-strokes—they get far better mileage. Significantly, they're also much kinder to the environment. They don't burn their lubricating oil, so they pollute much less.

1

Inside Your Engine— The Basic Components

This book isn't meant to turn you into an engine overhaul specialist, so we don't need to go into great detail about your engine's insides. You do, however, need to know where the most important major components are situated. That will help later, when you learn to "listen" for trouble. If abnormal noises come from your engine some day, you'll know what part is acting up.

It may seem surprising, but regardless of what brand of outboard engine you have, its internal layout will be essentially the same as any other brand's. You will find differences, though, between two-stroke and four-stroke engine internal configurations.

Figure 1-1 shows a typical two-stroke outboard engine with all the major parts identified. Figure 1-2 shows a new four-stroke outboard. The latter looks

(and in fact is) very much like a modern automobile engine tilted on end.

You'll note that one of the major differences between the two is that the four-stroke has valves on each cylinder: an intake valve to let the fuel/air mixture into the cylinder and an exhaust valve to allow the exhaust gases to escape. The opening and closing of these valves is controlled by a timing belt attached to the crankshaft.

This means, incidentally, that owners of four-strokes have some servicing tasks the two-stroke owner never has to deal with. One is the need for periodic inspection and replacement of the timing belt. Figure 1-2 shows how the belt connects the crankshaft (center), to the overhead camshaft (left) that, in turn, controls the valves.

Another maintenance task reserved for the four-stroke owner is to change the crankcase oil and filter

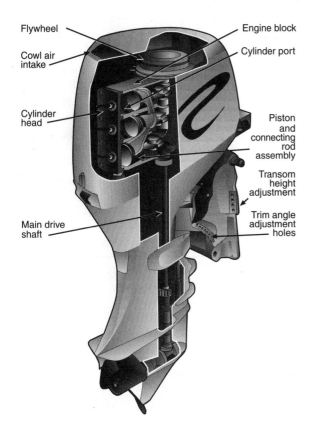

Figure 1-1. *Cutaway view of a typical two-stroke outboard engine.*

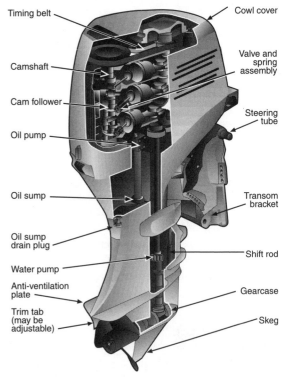

Figure 1-2. *Cutaway view of a typical four-stroke outboard engine.*

periodically—just as you do with your car. Two-stroke engines don't have crankcase oil, as we'll see later.

In addition, a four-stroke engine's valves will need adjustment now and then. A two-stroke gets along fine without valves—at the cost of reduced efficiency and increased pollution.

Don't worry if you haven't managed to absorb everything so far. It's not the detail we're studying here, just the basic principles. As you go through this book, the names and procedures will come up again, and you'll greet them like old friends. Meanwhile, take another look at Figures 1-1 and 1-2. They'll help you to visualize the parts mentioned.

Basic Two-Stroke and Four-Stroke Cycles

Most outboards are two-stroke engines, but as we move toward the 21st century, more and more four-stroke engines will appear. Each kind has its advantages and disadvantages but the four-stroke, with its cleaner exhaust emissions, will set the standard for the future. In any case, to be an engine troubleshooter you need to know how both kinds of engine work.

Remember the four basic needs; they can't be stressed enough. Whether it's a two-stroke or a four-stroke, the engine needs a fuel/air mixture delivered to the cylinder; it needs to compress it; the mixture must somehow be ignited; and, when it's done burning, the exhaust gases must be removed. This process occurs repeatedly as the engine runs, and the order in which these things happen must be exact to within a fraction of a second.

The Four-Stroke. It may help to think of an internal combustion engine as a pump of sorts. Let's take a look at Figure 1-3 to see how the four-stroke works:

Stroke 1—The piston travels down the cylinder, drawing the air-fuel mixture in behind it.

Stroke 2—On its way up again, the piston compresses this mixture to help make a more efficient explosion. (Incidentally, the piston rings stop the mixture from leaking out of the slight gap at the sides.)

Stroke 3—When it's nicely compressed, this mixture is ignited, and the resulting explosion forces the piston down the cylinder. The piston, as

we've mentioned before, has a connecting rod attached to an offset on the crankshaft, and that forces the crankshaft to turn.

Stroke 4—So, finally, while the piston is being pushed back to its starting position by the revolving crankshaft, it's also pushing out the burned gases and preparing to start the cycle all over again.

Thus, the engine has converted the reciprocating (back-and-forth) motion of the piston into something more useful for driving a propeller: rotary motion.

The Two-Stroke. Figure 1-4 depicts the two-stroke cycle. The significant difference here is the absence of conventional intake and exhaust valves. In fact, there are valves in a purely technical sense: The moving pistons alternately reveal and cover up ports (holes) in the cylinder wall, thus acting as valves. The ports are the means of gas entry and exit from the combustion chamber.

The other big difference is that the two-stroke engine actually combines the intake and compression strokes into one operation, and the power and exhaust strokes into another. As we've already seen, this enables it to complete all four necessary functions—intake, compression, ignition, and exhaust—with just two strokes of the piston in its cylinder, and only one revolution of the crankshaft instead of two.

Let's look at the sequence of events in Figure 1-4.

Diagram 1—The piston rises in the cylinder and compresses the air/fuel mixture on top of it. Note that the exhaust port (right) and intake port (left) have just been closed by the rising piston.

Diagram 2—As the piston rises and compresses the fuel mix, it also draws more fuel from the carburetor (bottom) into the crankcase.

Diagram 3—The piston begins its downward travel after the spark plug has ignited the compressed fuel mixture.

Diagram 4—The exhaust port (right) is uncovered, allowing the burned gases to escape. The downward-moving piston is also compressing the fuel mixture in the crankcase.

Diagram 5—Now the intake port also is being uncovered. The pressurized fuel mix bursts into the combustion chamber, forcing out the last of the exhaust gases and starting another sequence of compression and explosion.

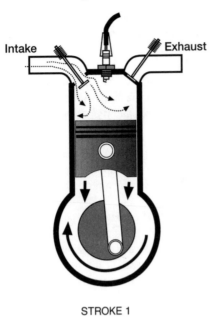

STROKE 1

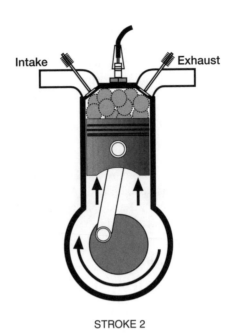

STROKE 2

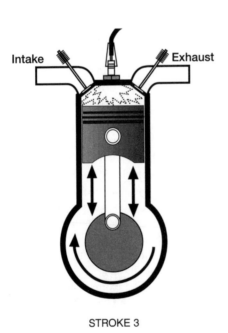

STROKE 3

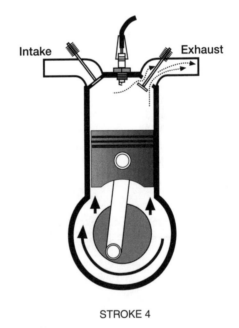

STROKE 4

Figure 1-3. *The four-stroke cycle illustrated. See text.*

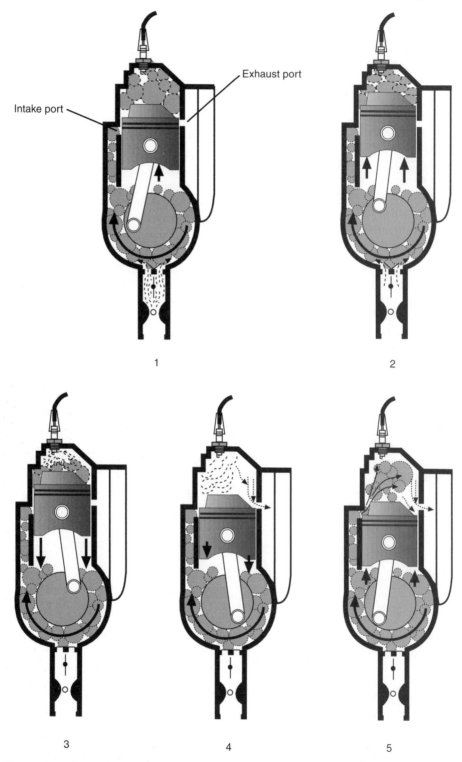

Figure 1-4. *The two-stroke cycle illustrated. See text.*

The Basics of Troubleshooting

While we're dealing with basic concepts, let's have a look at what I call the troubleshooting sequence. If your engine won't run, or is suddenly running poorly, you need to approach the problem in some sort of logical order. One of its basic needs, or sometimes more than one, is not being met. After you've read this book, you'll have the know-how to figure out which needs aren't being met, and how to correct the problem. You must consider all the possibilities, bearing in mind that some problems occur quite regularly, or at least are likely to happen after certain intervals. We'll delve into this in more detail later, but for the moment, here's a basic troubleshooting list for you to follow:

1. Think about the history of the engine and your problem. Is there anything you, or anyone else, may have done to cause the problem you are now experiencing? For example, did the problem crop up shortly after you refueled?
2. Do you have all the information you need to help solve the problem? Do you have your workshop manual, for example?
3. Start with simple solutions first. Visually inspect the whole system first. Look for leaks, corrosion, broken wires, or fittings. It may be that easy. Listen for, and isolate, any strange noises. Sniff around for fuel leaks, or burned wire insulation.
4. Once you've isolated the problem area or system, follow the steps outlined in the appropriate chapter of this book and, if necessary, use your engine manual as a supplement.
5. Have confidence in your test results and conclusions. Don't second-guess.
6. Repair the problem, and test your work for satisfactory outcome.

Incidentally, here's a tip to help you start your troubleshooting career: When you're working on your engine, learn to use your senses of sight, hearing, smell, and touch to pinpoint problems. And please learn to follow test procedures *completely,* from start to finish, and in a logical sequence. Don't short-circuit any procedures, no matter how sure you are that you've found the problem. It takes a little discipline to work this way, but if you can learn to do these things, you'll always be able to pinpoint the cause of any engine problem.

Meanwhile, you should use this chapter as a foundation on which to build. Remember, when your engine begins to act up, really knowing and understanding the basic information in these first few pages will go a long way toward pointing you in the right direction for a quick and economical repair, without replacing parts needlessly and wasting hours trying to come up with a logical repair plan.

A wise man once said, "Keep it simple." He was right. And correct maintenance is the way to do that. If you follow the guidelines I give for maintaining your engine, your problems will almost always be simple and easily put right.

Chapter 2

Breaking in a New Engine

Proper engine break-in is one of the keys to long engine life. Improper break-in can cause hidden damage to piston rings, crankshafts, and bearings. Gears and bearings can be chipped or burred if proper procedures are not followed. All manufacturers have a recommended "ritual" that must be followed to ensure warranty coverage of their engines.

The unfortunate truth is that improper break-in procedures can cause problems that may not show up on your engine until after the warranty period is over. The best advice is to follow closely the recommendations of the manufacturer or, in the case of a newly overhauled engine, the directions provided by the rebuilder.

Creating a generic break-in checklist is difficult because recommendations vary somewhat from one maker to another, but I can offer you some general guidelines.

General Break-in Guidelines

First and foremost, you must be certain that the fuel you use meets the minimum octane requirements as specified in your owner's manual. Most makers require at least the "regular" grade available in the U.S., with a minimum "69 RON" grade internationally. It is safe to assume that if your car will run on the available fuel, your outboard will as well.

One problem with fuel in some areas, however, has nothing to do with octane, but rather with the blending of alcohol in the fuel. OMC, for example, recommends not using any fuel with more than 10 percent alcohol, by volume. Reformulated or "oxygenated" fuels use alcohol, among other things, to meet government requirements in some parts of the U.S. How do you know what you're buying? In most cases, you really have no idea.

Excess alcohol in outboard engine fuel has been a problem for some manufacturers over the last 10 years. Alcohol deteriorated some of the rubber fuel hoses and internal carburetor parts, leading to plugged jets and a variety of other running problems. Some manufacturers now make parts that can withstand exposure to alcohol.

Technicians at Yamaha Motor Corporation recently told me that they have experienced no problems with their motors that can be attributed to this fuel blend. I have had problems with OMC products that can be blamed on alcohol in fuel, and experts working with the Mercury lines have told me that they too have had problems. The answer lies in whose engine you are running and when it was built. The newer engines are using components modified to withstand alcohol exposure.

If you suspect you are having problems caused by alcohol-rich fuel, ask your dealer to inquire about any service bulletins or factory recommendations. Rumors surrounding this topic are rampant, and often inaccurate.

Additives. Regarding "miracle" fuel additives that guarantee to clean your fuel system, remove carbon deposits, boost octane, and dry the gas—stay away! Use only manufacturer-recommended fuel conditioners that have been extensively tested on your type of engine. No matter what the label says, you have no assurance that the product has been tested with an engine like yours.

It's important to remember that the two-stroke outboard engine gets its lubrication exclusively from the mixture of fuel and oil, and you don't want to do anything that will alter tested chemical combinations. All the major manufacturers make additives, such as Yamaha's "Ring-Free" and OMC's "Carbon Guard," as well as stabilizers for extended storage. Use these additives only, and be sure to follow the instructions on the container.

Oil Grades. Another important consideration for proper engine break-in is the two-stroke oil itself. At this time, the highest grade of oil available is nominated TCW-3 by the Boating Industry Association (BIA). The TCW stands for Two-Cycle, Watercooled. Depending upon the age of your engine, your manual may recommend oil rated as TCW or TCW-2. (TCW and TCW-2 oils are no longer produced, but be cautious, some dealers might still have some old stock to sell.) But if you're breaking in an engine, either from new or after an overhaul, use TCW-3.

There have been many problems with larger engines in recent years concerning excess carbon build-up on piston and rings, leading to failure of these parts. These deposits of carbon are directly attributable to less-than-perfect fuel and oil formulations. Manufacturers have responded by advising you to use proprietary "engine tuner" solvents, and additives designed to remove this excess build-up in the combustion chambers. Take their advice if you want trouble-free operation. The new TCW-3 oil is designed to reduce combustion chamber deposits significantly.

Mix Ratio. In addition to selecting the correct grade of fuel and oil, the ratio of the mix is an important consideration during engine break-in. In general, manufacturers will recommend that the quantity of oil in the fuel be doubled during the break-in period; for example, from 50 to 1 to 25 to 1. This means 1 part of oil to each 50 parts, or 25 parts, of gasoline. (See page 80 for an oil-mixing chart to help you determine the correct amounts.) If your engine has an automatic oil-injection system, the manufacturer may recommend that you add oil in a specified ratio to your gasoline tank *in addition* to the oil in the engine's oil-injection reservoir.

Operating Procedure. How you operate your engine during the break-in period is also important. There are rules to follow. They vary from one manufacturer to another, so I can't give you a generic procedure that will be accurate for every engine. You must find out what the specific rules are for your engine, and follow them religiously. In general, however, the procedure is this:

- Don't let the engine idle for any extended period.
- Don't race the engine at maximum speed.
- Make sure cooling water is circulating by frequently checking the "telltale," or "tracer," spray—the water that squirts out behind the engine when the pump is working.
- If you have them, check engine instruments frequently for a normal operating temperature—about 145 to 155°F (63 to 68°C).
- Vary engine speed every 10 to 15 minutes; don't run the engine continuously at a steady speed.
- If you have a planing hull, use full throttle very briefly during the first hour—only to lift your boat onto a plane—and then back off to three-quarters throttle; but make sure the boat stays on the plane at this throttle position. If you have a displacement hull, don't use full throttle at all for the first hour if you can help it.
- After the first hour of operation, you may use full throttle for about a minute at a time once every 15 minutes or so.
- After 10 hours of operation, you will probably be required to take the engine back to your dealer or repair person for a final check and some adjustments. Consult your manual and your warranty, and be sure to follow the recommendations to the letter to ensure continued warranty coverage.
- After the break-in period, switch to a normal fuel/oil mix.

Chapter 3

Routine Maintenance

After your engine has been properly broken in, you'll need to establish a maintenance routine that begins with systematic checks every time you use your boat. These checks won't take long, but could spell the difference between life and death for your engine.

Daily Checks and Maintenance

Daily checks should include a quick look at just a few key items. See Figure 3-1.

First, make sure that your oil tank (if you have one) is topped up. If you have a four-stroke engine, be sure to check the crankcase-oil level and top up if needed. Check your owner's manual to determine if your dipstick should be screwed in, or left unthreaded when you check the oil level. Failure to do so could give you a false reading, and lead to overfilling or underfilling your engine's crankcase, which can cause problems.

Check that you have adequate fuel for your intended trip, and that the fuel-tank vent is open.

With the engine tilted up, check for excess oil buildup near your propeller—it could mean that a seal in your lower gearcase has deteriorated. (Note: Some oil film buildup is normal in many cases; look for changes in the amount of buildup. If it appears to be increasing, check the oil level in the lower unit as discussed in the owner's manual or in Chapter 9.) If the seal has failed, take the engine to a repair shop immediately to avoid expensive gear-unit damage.

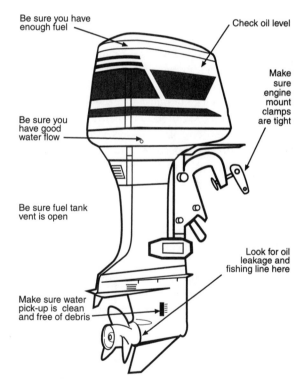

Figure 3-1. *Typical points to check daily.*

Check for fishing line wrapped around the propeller hub area. If you ignore it, the line can wrap tightly around the propshaft and cause the aforementioned gearcase seal failure.

If your engine is not through-bolted to the transom of your boat, make sure the screw clamps are tight and secure. Many engines have landed on the bottom of the lake through neglect of this simple check.

Sniff around for any sign of a fuel leak, and if you find one, fix it.

Once the engine is running, make sure to check the "telltale," or "tracer," spray, or exhaust discharge, to be certain the water pump is working.

If all these items are in order, you're ready to go. There's just one more thing:

If you tow your boat on a trailer, and run it in salt water, flush the cooling system daily with fresh water. See Chapter 9 for details.

Monthly Checks and Maintenance

On a monthly basis, besides the routine daily checks, it's a good idea to remove the engine cover and look for any corrosion build-up near cylinder heads and thermostat housings that could indicate leaky gaskets. They must be attended to—see Figure 3-2. Also, look for corrosion at wire terminal connections—clean and tighten them as required and then use one of the proprietary anti-corrosion sprays available at your dealership on all exposed electrical connections and unpainted metal parts of your engine.

Make sure that throttle and gear-shift controls operate smoothly. Lubricate them as needed. Be aware that you should never shift gears unless your engine is running, so make sure the boat is securely made fast to the dock before checking shift controls for smooth operation.

Next, run the engine with the cover off and check that none of the bolt-on components (fuel pumps, voltage regulators, coils, and the like) have come loose from their mounts. Make sure all wires and cables are securely led and clipped through harness mounts.

Next, if your engine is equipped with an engine-mounted fuel strainer, check to see if any water has collected in it. It will be easy to see, as the water will separate from the fuel, drop to the bottom of the strainer, and be relatively clear in color compared to the fuel/oil mix above it. Figure 3-3 shows what it looks like.

If you can see water, remove the strainer housing and drain out the water. Clean the screen element, reinstall, making sure the O-ring is in place before

threading the housing back in, and re-check this assembly for fuel leaks after replacing the strainer housing. Simply pump your fuel primer bulb until the filter/strainer fills with fuel, and look for leaking fuel.

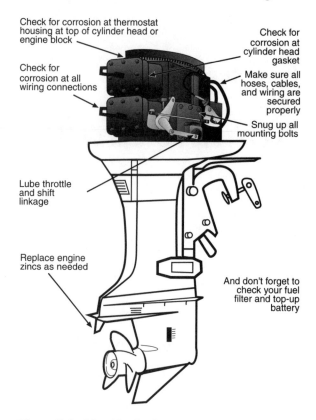

Figure 3-2. *Monthly check points.*

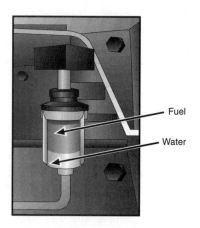

Figure 3-3. *Separation of water and gasoline in a fuel strainer.*

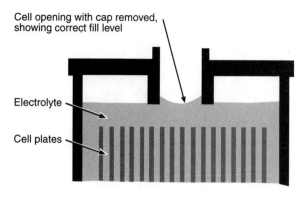

Cell opening with cap removed, showing correct fill level

Electrolyte

Cell plates

Figure 3-4. *Correct battery cell fill level.*

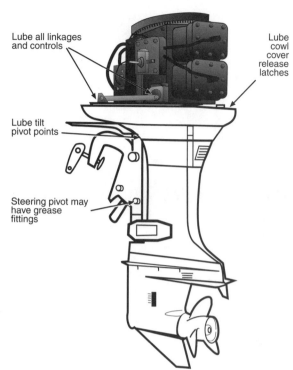

Lube all linkages and controls

Lube cowl cover release latches

Lube tilt pivot points

Steering pivot may have grease fittings

Figure 3-5. *Typical lubrication points.*

Next, you should check the condition of any sacrificial zinc anodes attached to your engine. Check for zincs at the lower portion of the mounting bracket on larger engines. There may be a zinc trim tab behind the propeller, or a small zinc screwed onto the anti-ventilation plate. Replace any zincs that are more than half eroded. In some areas they can dissolve quite rapidly, and if the zincs are completely gone, the only thing left to dissolve is your engine housing.

Lastly, check your engine's battery, and top up the cells as needed. See Figure 3-4.

Seasonal Checks and Maintenance

First let's define the word "seasonal." The way I apply it here, it actually means every three months, or every full boating season, whichever comes first. In other words, if you can boat all the year round, or for more than three months anyway, do these checks and maintenance procedures at least once every three months, or about every 50 to 75 hours of operation.

But if you live in a region where your boat use is restricted to less than three months, or 75 hours, consider these "seasonal" checks to be annual checks.

Three-Month (or Seasonal) Service Checks

Seasonal check-ups are far more comprehensive, and certain operations may require the expertise of your local dealer, but you'll certainly be able to do all of the work listed here except in the few cases I've noted.

Grease Points. All grease points on your engine should be filled with fresh grease as recommended by your manufacturer for the specific engine location. Keep pumping in grease until all the old grease—and any water—is forced out. It's a messy business, so wipe the old stuff away with a rag as it emerges around the lube point. See Figure 3-5 for the grease points commonly found on most engines.

Propeller Inspection. First, be certain your ignition system is disabled by disconnecting the spark plug wires at the plugs. Then remove the propeller to inspect the shaft for any fishing line wrapped around it. If you find any, cut it all off.

Inspect the propeller for nicks, burrs, and any unwanted bends in the propeller blades. If the nicks are minor, you can clean them up with a file.

Inspect the propeller hub for any deterioration of the vulcanized rubber and its attachment to the hub spline. Any damage found here could spell trouble next season. If this hub is damaged, you'll need either to

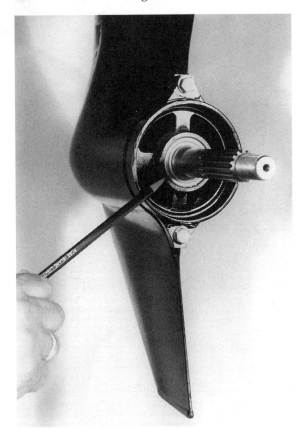

Figure 3-6. *Propeller shaft and outer oil seal.*

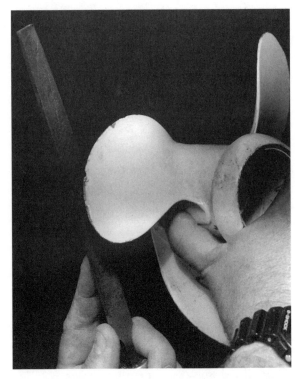

Figure 3-7. *Filing out a nick in a propeller.*

Figure 3-8. *Vulcanized propeller hub being inspected.*

have the prop rehubbed or a new prop. If you're in doubt, have your dealer make the final call. You certainly don't want to replace it if you don't have to.

If all looks okay here, wipe down the propeller shaft to remove the old grease, and apply a thin coat of an approved waterproof grease to the shaft. Don't reinstall the propeller just yet, as you're going to run the engine to flush the cooling system, and you should never run an engine out of the water with the propeller on because of the obvious danger from the whirring blades.

When you do reinstall the propeller however, remember to replace the cotter pin for the prop nut if your engine is equipped with one. If your engine uses a Nylock self-locking prop nut, it should be replaced, as these lock effectively only once.

Figure 3-6 shows a typical propeller shaft and seal

assembly, the splines to be greased, and the seal to inspect for any fishing line fouling.

Figure 3-7 shows a minor nick being filed off the edge of a propeller blade.

Figure 3-8 points out the vulcanized prop hub being inspected for cracks and any breakdown in the vulcanization between the propeller and the hub itself.

Gearcase-Oil Change.
The next step in the seasonal service process is to change the gearcase oil. On most outboards, the gearcase will have two screw plugs evident in the side of the gear housing. Some engines, however, will have the gear unit's drain and fill screws located on the hub just forward of the propeller, in which case they can only be reached with the propeller removed. Figure 3-9 shows the typical locations of the drain plug (bottom) and the level-check plug.

Figure 3-10. *Gearcase oil drains down masking tape.*

Figure 3-9. *Lower gearcase level-check plug and drain plug.*

To drain the fluid from your unit, wipe the skeg clean at the very bottom of the engine and attach a piece of masking tape to the skeg as shown in Figure 3-10.

Get a clean container that's large enough to hold all the oil in your gearcase and place it under the tape. Remove the lower drain plug. Nothing much will come out until you slowly unscrew the upper check plug. The oil will then leak down the side of the gear housing, down the side of the skeg, and flow straight down the edge of the tape into your drain pan.

Carefully inspect the oil for excessive metal filings or discoloration. If the oil appears milky, or if you noticed a large amount of water coming out of the drain before the oil, then water has somehow migrated into the gearcase, indicating a bad seal. In that case, you should remove the lower unit, following the procedures outlined in Chapter 9, and take it to your dealer. Ask to have the assembly checked for pressure and vacuum, and have the appropriate seals replaced.

If the drained oil appears to be a normal medium brown to dark brown, or in some cases green, with few metal filings in it (some are normal), then inspect the drain-plug sealing rings and replace them if they're damaged.

Clean off the magnetic pickup found on many lower drain plugs and get ready to refill the lower unit with the correct gear oil.

A note of caution here: Don't let anyone talk you into using straight gear oil as supplied by auto parts stores. Although this oil may have the same distinctive rotten egg odor as the fluid you have just removed from your outboard engine, it may not be the same stuff. Typically, the special outboard engine gear oils have a water-dispersant additive in them that's not found in the automotive grades. Also, be aware that not all outboards use gear oil in their gearcases. Some use four-stroke engine oil, and others use a fluid quite similar to automotive automatic transmission oil. Be sure to check the specifications for your engine. It's best to go to your dealer to purchase a container of the correct oil and one of the special fill pumps shown in Figure 3-11.

These pumps are quite inexpensive and fit not only the oil container, but screw directly into the threaded lower unit drainplug hole on your engine, minimizing mess. This is an important point, because you're going to fill the gearcase from the bottom up. Once you are set-up as shown in Figure 3-11, simply work the pump until you just begin to see oil seeping from the top check-plug hole. Then reinstall the check plug and snug up the screw.

Next, get the drain/fill plug ready to install, wipe down the magnetic pickup, and be sure the sealing O-ring or gasket is either in place on the screw plug or in the gear housing. Unscrew the pump tool and quickly insert the drain/fill plug. Tighten it fully. Wipe off any excess oil from the gearcase and watch for leaks. Your oil change is complete.

Cooling System. The next step in the seasonal service is to thoroughly flush your cooling system with fresh water. Follow the procedure as outlined in Chapter 9, covering cooling systems and lower units. A precaution here is to make certain that the flush adapter stays in place while you are flushing the engine. If the adapter slides down on the lower unit to a point below the water inlet, you could burn out the engine's water pump—or the engine itself—if it's left unattended for even a brief time. Figure 3-12 shows the cooling system flush adapter attached and ready to go.

As part of this cooling system service, it's also a good idea to remove and clean your engine's thermostat, if it has one. The internal cavity into which the thermostat and bypass valve fits is a trap for sand, salt, and general debris that gets past the system pickup strainer. With the thermostat removed, clean out any muck you find there and, with the engine running, run fresh water up from the flushing adapter through the engine to this point. You'll now know for certain that the internal water flow is unrestricted, because water will leak out at this point. Just run the engine long enough to determine that a good solid flow of water is pouring out.

After the thermostat has been cleaned, reinstall it, using new gaskets, and run the engine again to be sure

Figure 3-11. *Pumping fresh oil into the gearcase.*

Figure 3-12. *Muffs attached for engine flushing.*

the thermostat cover is not leaking. Figure 3-13 shows the thermostat removed for inspection and cleaning. Chapter 9 details testing of a thermostat to determine normal operation. If your engine has seemed to be run-

ning too hot lately, but your inspection has now revealed that water is getting to this point in adequate amounts, the operation of the thermostat could be the problem.

Impeller Replacement. In addition to flushing the cooling system and checking the thermostat, you may also regard the replacement of your water-pump impeller as routine maintenance. To tell the truth, manufacturer's recommendations vary on this score, some suggesting that you renew the impeller every year, and others that you replace it only as needed.

My advice is to replace the impeller yearly if you run your engine in an area where you draw sand through the system regularly. Also, if you regularly venture far offshore, where failure of the water pump could be a serious problem, replace that impeller yearly.

On the other hand, if you use your motor only occasionally throughout the season, or on a tender, for non-risky trips from ship to shore, I'd advise you to replace the impeller every other year. Again, Chapter 9 explains this procedure in detail.

Cylinder Compression. Now that you've run your engine for a bit to flush your cooling system, and have warmed it up, it's a good idea to perform the annual compression test. Remember, compression is one of your engine's basic needs and a compression check can often catch impending problems before they become major.

For example, piston rings that are just beginning to gum up will cause low compression before they fail completely. Usually, you can cure this problem by running a manufacturer-approved decarbonizing fluid such as OMC or Mercury "Engine Tuner" through the engine. If you don't catch this problem in time, the only solution is to take the engine apart. It's simple to use these engine tuners—the instructions are right there on the product label.

What's often not so easy is finding out what normal compression is for your engine. Often the specs are not given in the engine owner's manual or even in the workshop service manual. So it's a good idea to check the compression when the engine is fairly new and in good running order. Write down the compression figures for each cylinder in your manual for future reference.

Figure 3-13. *Thermostat removed for cleaning and inspection.*

As a matter of interest, the actual pressure is not that important—it's the variation from the norm that you should be concerned with. In the case of a multi-cylinder engine, start worrying if any one cylinder varies from the others by 15 pounds per square inch (psi) or more. If yours is a single-cylinder engine, a drop of 15 psi from the norm you established when it was new is cause for concern. The steps for performing a compression test are really quite simple, but you must follow them exactly for your own safety and the accuracy of the readings. So be warned—don't skip any of these steps:

1. First, disable the ignition system by unplugging the gang plug going into your ignition module. If your engine has an emergency shut-off switch, simply remove the lanyard clip to disable the ignition. If neither of these solutions works on your engine, take a wire jumper lead and connect one end to a good engine ground, and the other end to the metal connector inside the spark plug boot. You'll have to use one jumper for each plug wire. Remember, simply disconnecting all the plug wires may be a dangerous move. Once you remove all your spark plugs and begin cranking over your engine, an explosive fuel/oil mix will be spraying out of the plug holes. A plug wire could spark and ignite this mix outside of the combustion chamber if it isn't grounded to the engine. Also, this freewheeling type of spark could damage the ignition coils or modules.

2. Remove all the spark plugs, and be sure to keep them in order so you can return them to the cylinders they came from. Carefully inspect the business end of the plugs, looking for any inconsistency in coloration, and for any sign of water or rust near the tip.

3. Next, thread your compression gauge into the #1 spark-plug hole and "zero" the gauge.

4. Open the throttle as far as possible, to ensure that the cylinder gets an unrestricted supply of air. (Some engines allow only minimal opening if the gearshift is in neutral, to guard against over-revving.)

5. Crank over the engine an equal number of times for each cylinder you test, and be sure to re-zero the gauge for each cylinder. If you have an electric start, count the seconds: "One thousand one, one thousand two, one thousand three, one thousand four" and so on, with the key or start button engaged. This will give you enough cranking time for a usable reading. If you have a pull start, pull the cord four to five times for each cylinder you are testing.

6. Record your readings from each cylinder for future reference. Use the 15 psi criterion already mentioned to determine if further action is required.

If compression readings are lower than normal for any cylinders, try a "wet" compression test, which will temporarily seal the piston rings, and determine if they are the cause of the low reading.

To perform this test, get a can of your favorite fogging oil and insert the red nozzle tube in the push button. Now carefully insert the other end of the tube into the spark plug hole and spray into the cylinder with a circular motion to distribute oil spray all around the perimeter of the piston. Spray for about four seconds.

Remove the nozzle and install your compression tester. Spin the engine over exactly the same number of times you did for the previous test and compare your gauge readings. If the compression rises noticeably, then your rings are beginning to stick.

If you've caught the problem early enough, decarbonizing with an "engine tuner" fluid, as described above, may cure it. If the dry compression was really low, and no change is evident during the wet test, it's too late. Your rings and/or piston are worn to the point where major engine disassembly will be required. So be brave, and consult your dealer.

If two adjacent cylinders on a multicylinder engine give a similarly low reading, or if there was evidence of water or rust on the spark plugs from these cylinders, then the problem is a faulty head gasket. This is usually a problem better left for a professional to deal with, but if you have enough engine experience, you may want to tackle it yourself.

Incidentally, beware of compression readings from an engine that has been in storage for an extended period. While it's sitting idle, the piston rings will "relax" and retract slightly, often giving an initially low and misleading reading. Always run an engine to operating temperature to ensure that the reading you get is

Figure 3-14. *A compression test in progress.*

accurate. Figure 3-14 shows a compression tester installed and ready to go on an outboard engine.

One last tip—if the spark plugs have been in the engine for the entire season, now's the time to replace them in accordance with the guidelines outlined in Chapter 5 covering ignition systems.

Fuel System. The next phase of the annual inspection is to thoroughly check your boat's entire fuel system for any signs of leaks, loose clamps, or cracked, frayed hoses and squeeze bulbs. Any rust patches on your fuel tanks should be sanded and touched up. Also, inspect the venting system for your fuel tank. It should be free to breathe. Any restriction can stop your engine.

An easy way to check for a fuel leak from the primer bulb to the engine is to squeeze the bulb until it gets firm, and hold pressure on it to be certain it remains firm while the engine's not running. If it doesn't stay firm, there's a leak in the system between the bulb and the engine, or in the engine itself at the carburetor or fuel pump.

You may have to remove some access panels on your boat to do a visual check of the whole fuel delivery system, but don't neglect this important task. Figure 3-15 shows the typical annual fuel system checkpoints for boats with portable and permanent fuel tanks.

Automatic Oiler. Your next job is to check the automatic oil-blending system, if your engine is so equipped. Clean and inspect all lines and connections, replacing any cracked lines and tightening loose connections as required. It's a good idea to check with your dealer for specific recommendations for your engine. On some engines, oil delivery pump diaphragms

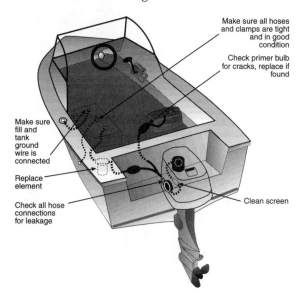

Make sure all hoses and clamps are tight and in good condition

Check primer bulb for cracks, replace if found

Make sure fill and tank ground wire is connected

Replace element

Check all hose connections for leakage

Clean screen

Figure 3-15. *Fuel system inspection points.*

should be replaced as part of an annual service. Also, have a good look at the oil reservoir filter screen, and clean it or replace it. More detailed information regarding the various oiling systems is found in Chapter 7 of this book.

Steering. Your boat's steering system needs to be thoroughly inspected at least once a year, but don't hesitate to see what's amiss any time you feel unusual looseness or tightness in the steering wheel. Inspect steering cables for any signs of separation, cracks in the outer sheathing, or rust buildup near the cable ends. More details, and key service points for this system, are given in Chapter 8.

Battery. Next, check and clean all battery-cable connections and battery tops. Smear a light coating of Vaseline or similar light grease over the tightened connection. Top up the cells to the level indicated in Figure 3-4. If you're planning to put the boat in storage, remove the battery and trickle-charge it every month.

Two Final Adjustments. Last, you should have your dealer set your ignition timing, and adjust your carburetor(s). These are not procedures the part-time mechanic should attempt on an outboard engine. There are simply too many expensive tools required in many

cases, and the damage that can be caused by improper settings can be catastrophic. So, unless you have considerable experience with engines, stay away from these two adjustments.

Special Considerations for Four-Stroke Engines

In addition to everything already discussed, four-stroke outboard engines add three more maintenance tasks to the list:

Sump-Oil Change. Four-stroke engines have an oil sump, and use a pressurized lubrication system like the one in your car. Depending on the make and model, your four-stroke may even use a spin-on type oil filter, just as your car engine does.

Changing your engine's sump oil is fairly simple, but even here there are several tricks of the trade that will make life easier. I'll discuss them as we go along.

Before you do anything, warm the engine up. This makes the old oil thinner and runnier, and helps it drain out of the engine sump.

Once the engine is nice and warm, locate the oil drain plug. Your manual will help you if you don't know where it is. On some engines, you may have to unscrew an access panel located on the mid-section of the engine. Figure 1-2 (page 2) shows the usual location. Once you've found the right plug, find a container the old oil can drain into.

Now, unscrew the drain plug, and make sure the sealing ring for the plug comes off with the plug so you don't lose it in the drain oil. Inspect this sealing ring, and if it looks crushed get a new one. Inspect the oil as it's draining. In particular, keep an eye open for any milky discoloration. That's a sign that water has seeped into the oil, and should be checked out immediately. Usually, it's caused by a cylinder-head gasket that is leaking internally, allowing cooling water to enter the crankcase section of the engine block. Have it fixed now, or face severe engine damage in the near future.

When all the oil has drained, wipe off any spillage with a clean cloth and reinstall the drain plug.

CAUTION: Most amateurs tend to over-tighten oil drain plugs. Remember, this plug is being screwed into threads well lubricated with drained oil. It will screw in very easily, making over-torquing all too likely.

Snug is the operative word here, not tight. Over-tightening could make the plug virtually impossible to remove at the next oil change.

The next step in the oil-change process is to remove and clean the oil strainer or spin-on filter if your engine is so equipped. Yamaha and the smaller Honda four-strokes use a strainer screen that is simply unthreaded from the engine and washed out in a mild solvent such as mineral spirits or kerosene. Inspect the strainer for any damage and replace it if needed. Otherwise, just reinstall it.

If your engine has a spin-on filter element, as the new Johnsons and larger Hondas do, there are several precautions you should follow. First, you will spin the filter off by hand, turning the element in a counterclockwise direction. If the element is too tight (which is often the case), you may have to add a special oil-filter wrench to your arsenal of tools. These wrenches come in several sizes and configurations, but get the smallest wrench your auto parts store sells. I have found the strap type with a pivoting handle to be the most useful in small spaces.

As the filter comes loose, and as it gets near the end of the threads holding it to the engine, tip the face of the element upwards to avoid spilling oil all over your engine. That makes for a messy clean-up project.

Once you've got the filter element off, check to see that the filter sealing ring came off with the element, and isn't still stuck to the engine block. Screwing a new element onto an old ring is a sure way to create a massive oil leak. Now wipe up the oil that spilled despite your best efforts.

Next, put a light coating of engine oil on the sealing ring of the new filter element and carefully thread it onto the engine. As with drain plugs, the tendency is to over-tighten filters. The procedure here is to thread the element onto the engine until the sealing ring makes firm contact with the engine block surface, and snug it up an additional half to three-quarters of a turn—no more! Finally, make sure the engine is in a level, normal operating position, and add the amount of fresh oil specified by your engine maker.

Run the engine for a minute or so to fill the new filter, and check for any leaks. Shut the engine down, and recheck the oil level in the crankcase. Make sure not to overfill the crankcase as this is a sure-fire way to overload crankcase seals, causing oil leaks you never had before.

Timing-Belt Wear.   At least once a season, it's a good idea to check your four-stroke engine's timing belt for excessive wear. Figure 3-16 shows the timing belt side clearance being checked on a new four-stroke Yamaha engine.

Outboard manufacturers now recommend that belts be replaced only when needed, and not at fixed intervals. Based on experience with some of the older Honda engines and the small Yamaha units, this replacement interval will be measured in years, many years. But it pays to be safe, so you should inspect annually for any sign of fraying or excessive side-to-side play in the belt—anything greater than $1/2$ inch (13 mm) would indicate a need for replacement. Note that to get to the belt, you'll have to remove the plastic protective cover over the flywheel and timing gear on the very top of the engine. This is a simple case of removing a few screws, and in some cases a pin, located on the front of the engine.

Valve Clearance Check.   The last consideration for owners of four-stroke outboards is the need to check engine valve clearances periodically. Manufacturers recommend that you do this after every 100 hours of operation or at six-monthly intervals, so I've included it as part of the seasonal checklist.

Valve adjustment sounds a lot harder to do than it really is, but it still requires careful following of the procedures outlined in your workshop manual. If you have no experience with engines, or you find your workshop manual more confusing than helpful, it's best to let your dealer do this job, especially as improper adjustment can cause serious engine damage.

An important thing to remember about valve adjustment is that most people associate improper adjustment with a ticking noise coming from the valve cover. It's true that this ticking noise can be made by a loosely adjusted cam follower, but the fact is that most valve misadjustments make no abnormal noises at all. You can't assume that just because your engine seems to be running fine, and there's no ticking noise from the valve cover, you can skip this part of the maintenance routine.

Many valves actually get tighter as they wear into the cylinder head, eventually reaching a point where they fail to seat properly, which causes premature burning of the valve head.

Here's the general procedure for valve adjustment:

Figure 3-16. *Checking the timing belt for wear.*

Remove the valve cover. Remove the spark plugs so the engine can't kick over as you work.

You'll need to find the piston's top dead center, on the compression stroke, for the cylinder you're working on. Figure 1-3, Stroke 3 (page 4) shows a piston how you want it. At this point, the piston is at the top of its travel, and both intake and exhaust valves are fully closed. This is the point where the valve "lash" is at its maximum and should be checked and adjusted as needed. Figure 3-17 shows the correct feeler gauge installed with the adjustment screw locknut backed off and the screw being adjusted.

This "lash" is simply an air gap between the valve and the lever (rocker arm) that forces the valve to open and close. Lash is engineered into the valve opening and closing system to allow for expansion and contraction of the metals due to changes in the engine's operating temperature. Lash also ensures that the valves can

close completely at high engine rpm, when the inertia of the rapidly moving valves and rocker arms can actually allow them to "bounce" against each other.

You may need to take some special considerations into account for your particular engine. For a start, consult your manual about whether the engine needs to be hot or cold when you make the valve adjustments.

Find out, too, if the intake and exhaust valves have different clearance specs. Often the exhaust valves are set slightly looser than the intake valves.

And last, be very clear on whether the clearance specifications given in your manual are in thousandths of an inch or in hundredths of a millimeter—it makes a huge difference in terms of final clearance. Most feeler-gauge sets available today have both numbers embossed on the individual feeler leaves.

After your valve adjustment is complete, install a new gasket for the valve cover and reinstall the hold-

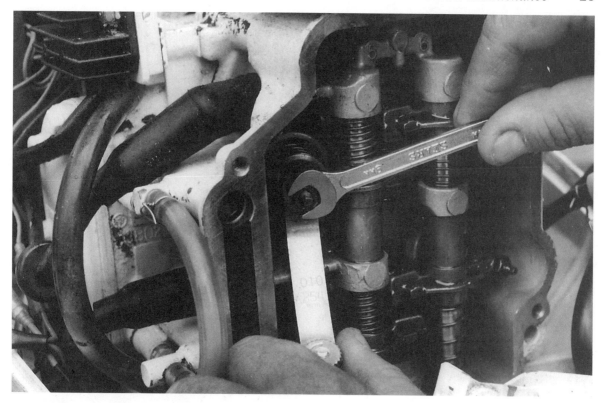

Figure 3-17. *Checking valve clearances.*

down screws, tightening them gradually and evenly, starting from the center-most screws and working toward the ends of the cover.

Maintenance in a Nutshell

The following tables summarize the information in this chapter. They provide a quick, easy-to-follow maintenance schedule for your engine.

Following the steps outlined here will help ensure that your engine gives you years of trouble-free service, and will enable you to discover developing problems early enough to make effective repairs before they become major.

Daily Checks

1. Check oil injection reservoir and top up as needed. For four-stroke engines, check crankcase oil level.

2. Check fuel tank level.
3. Open fuel tank vent.
4. Check propeller for fishing line or oil seepage.
5. Tighten engine mount clamp screws.
6. Check for and correct any fuel leaks.
7. Verify water pump operation by checking tracer, or telltale, spray.

Monthly Checks

1. Check for corrosion at cylinder head gasket, thermostat housing, and electrical connections.
2. Check shift and throttle linkage, lube as needed.
3. Check mounting screws for tightness on all powerhead-mounted accessories.
4. Check all wires, cables, and hoses to make sure they lead correctly and are secure.
5. Check fuel strainer and clean or replace as needed.
6. Check all zinc anodes and replace as needed.

7. Check battery connections and top up battery cells.

Seasonal Checks

1. Lube all engine grease points.
2. Remove propeller, inspect prop shaft and lubricate, check propeller blades and hub.
3. Change gearcase oil.
4. Flush cooling system.
5. Clean and inspect thermostat.
6. Inspect water pump impeller, replace as needed.
7. Check engine compression.
8. Replace spark plugs.
9. Inspect fuel system.
10. Inspect oil-injection system.
11. Inspect steering system.
12. Clean battery connections and top up cells.
13. Have dealer set ignition timing.
14. Have dealer set carburetor(s).

Additional Four-Stroke Annual Service

1. Change engine oil.
2. Service engine oil filter, replace if needed.
3. Check timing belt.
4. Adjust engine valve clearances.

Off-Season Storage and Spring Commissioning

The procedures for off-season storage have changed in recent years and really make the spring commissioning procedure much simpler as well as ensuring longer engine life. In addition to all the items already mentioned in the seasonal or annual service recommendations, you need to protect the internal components of your engine during winter storage. If you follow the procedures below, you'll enjoy longer engine life and an easy start-up next spring.

Winter Storage.   A good way to start is by stabilizing the fuel in your tanks. For that you need a "fuel conditioner." Each manufacturer has its own brand of fuel conditioner that's specifically made for your engine type, so stick to the recommended brand. Simply add the correct amount of stabilizer to your fuel, as directed on the label, if you're not going to be using it for more than a month or so. It stops the fuel mixture from turning to harmful varnish in your carburetor and inside the engine.

Now you have to run your engine to draw the stabilized fuel right through the whole system. But before you start up, attach the fresh-water flushing muffs and remove the prop.

Run the engine at about 1,500 rpm for about five minutes to be certain the stabilized fuel reaches the carburetor float chambers. Then switch off your engine.

The next step is to remove the carburetor air-intake cover. Find your can of storage fogging oil and start the engine again. Now spray fogging oil into each carburetor throat until you can see heavy exhaust smoke and the engine begins to run roughly, nearly at a stall. At this point shut the engine down. Figure 3-18 shows fogging oil being sprayed down the carburetor throat.

Figure 3-18. *Spraying fogging oil into carburetor intake.*

Tools You'll Need

Every boater needs a basic tool kit, and if you're going to maintain and repair your outboard engine, you may want to expand your existing kit with some specialized items that will make your work much easier.

To begin, you are going to need the basics: screwdrivers, both slotted and Phillips; pliers; wire terminal crimpers/cutters; combination wrenches; sockets; and a hammer and some miscellaneous small punches.

You'll need to find out if your engine uses U.S. or metric fasteners and get the correct wrenches and sockets. Don't assume that because you have a Mercury or Johnson/Evinrude engine the nuts and bolts are American. Many of these engines are actually built overseas and use metric hardware.

For some tasks, you'll need a fairly large open-ended wrench (over 1 inch), so rather than buy an expensive set of these large wrenches, get an adjustable wrench that will open to about 1½ inches.

You'll also need a spark-plug gapping gauge, and if you have a four-stroke outboard, the appropriate feeler-gauge set for checking valve-clearance adjustments, and possibly a special socket wrench for making the adjustment. Check your manual for this information. Yamaha's valve-adjustment wrench part number is YM-08035/90890-01311.

You should also purchase a small grease gun at your local auto parts store, and ask for a needlepoint adapter for the end of it. You'll need it for some of the fittings on your engine.

In addition to the basics, you're going to have to add a multimeter (VOM), a spark tester, and for some of the more advanced ignition tests, a Quicksilver DVA adapter, part number 91-89045, available through Mercury engine dealers.

It's a good idea to have on hand jumper leads (lengths of insulated wire about 12 inches long with alligator clips at each end) for each cylinder of your engine.

Also, you will need to purchase a cooling system flushing adapter, or "muffs," for your engine at a local dealer or marine accessory supplier.

Last, it's a good idea to have an inexpensive compression tester in your collection, but if you don't want to purchase one, many auto parts stores rent them for a very small fee. Be sure to get the screw-in type, to ensure the most reliable readings in your testing.

This list will give you everything you need for all the procedures described in this book. More advanced work would require torque wrenches of several sizes, some special pullers, and meters for specialized electrical test procedures. These tools are quite expensive, and are better left to the pros. All the tools you need are shown in Figure 3-19.

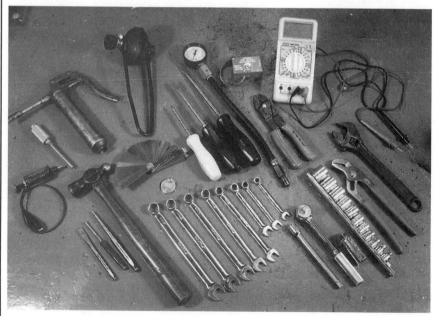

Figure 3-19.
Recommended tool kit.

After shutting down the engine, remove the spark plugs and spray fogging oil into each cylinder for about four seconds. Next, slowly turn the engine's flywheel over by hand to distribute the fogging oil to all parts of the cylinders. Reinstall the spark plugs, replacing them if necessary—see Chapter 5. Reinstall the air-intake cover.

If the engine has a portable fuel tank, it should now be removed and stored in a safe, well-ventilated place. Make sure to screw the vent closed.

If your boat has a built-in tank, it should be left nearly full with stabilized fuel. Tape over the hull-mounted vent for the winter to minimize condensation in the tank.

Next, you should lightly sand, prime, and touch up any chipped paint on the engine following the recommendations in Chapter 10. After you've done this, reinstall the engine cover and thoroughly wash the engine with soap and water. Finally, wax the entire unit using any good grade of automotive wax.

Your engine is now ready for its winter rest.

Spring Commissioning.

If you've followed all of the procedures outlined here for extended engine lay-up, your spring commissioning tasks will be simple, at least as far as your engine goes. All you'll need to do is reinstall your battery (fully charged), get the engine to the water (or attach your flushing muffs), and fire it up.

Don't be alarmed if a lot of smoke spews from the exhaust. It's the fogging oil burning off. It should all be gone in no more than about five minutes.

Chapter 4

How to Find the Trouble

Even the best-maintained engines run into trouble occasionally. You may pick up a bad tank of fuel, or marine growths may block the engine-cooling passages and cause it to overheat. General wear and tear will eventually take its toll. When it happens, your job is to pinpoint the source of trouble quickly and home in on a solution. To accomplish this, you'll need to use all of your senses, and follow a logical plan.

We'll come to the plan in a bit, but first you should consider the engine's history. What has been done to it recently? Or not been done to it, that should have been? Think hard about any service work that may have been performed. It's possible that something was overlooked or not done properly.

I can't tell you how many times I've seen engines over the years that "wouldn't go" simply because the propeller fell off. Somebody forgot to reinstall the locking cotter pin and the nut simply backed off. History is as important with engines as it is with the human body. One of the first things a doctor wants to know about you is your age. Why? Because the doctor knows that certain of your "parts" are likely to wear out with age, and some sooner than others if you've abused them. Your engine is no different in this respect.

Listen, Look, and Feel for Trouble

Every engine has its own characteristic sound. Every time you shift into forward or reverse, you'll hear a familiar "clunk" as the selected gear engages. You'll know the sounds made as you steer your boat from hard-over on one side to hard-over on the other. The whining noise your electric trim motor and pump mechanism make become quite normal. It pays to listen carefully to these and other noises to establish a mental reference for what's right and normal. Then, the instant you hear anything abnormal, you'll know something has gone wrong and be able to react quickly.

An excellent method for pinpointing noises is shown in Figure 4-1. If you put the handle of a long screwdriver to your ear as shown, you can use the tip as a probe to isolate the source of abnormal noises to within an extremely small area. The only precautions here are to be careful of touching moving parts on the engine while you listen, and to make sure your hair won't suddenly get blown into the moving machinery.

For some checks you may need a helper to operate the suspicious system while you probe with the screwdriver. You may eventually find that the source of the noise is in an area you really don't feel comfortable working with (such as inside the engine block), but at least you can go to a mechanic and provide an educated explanation. You can offer a lot more than a simple, "My boat's making a strange noise." And that can save you very expensive labor dollars that may otherwise have to be spent on isolating the strange noise.

Your sense of hearing is undoubtedly an invaluable troubleshooting tool, but another sense that approaches

Figure 4-1. *Using a screwdriver to pinpoint noises.*

it in value is sight. To make best use of it, you first need to know what "normal" looks like. Then you'll be better able to spot trouble signs and know what they could mean. You'll get varying degrees of help in this area from owner's manuals and factory service manuals, depending upon the manufacturer. With or without the manual, you should train yourself to pay a great deal of attention to detail. It's very important.

For example, Figure 4-2 shows a very simple visual check. You can actually see that fuel is getting all the way to the carburetor. Establishing this fact eliminates a multitude of possibilities as shown on the troubleshooting chart that follows.

Corrosion is one of the most common problems you can track down with your eyes, and it can affect many systems. Figure 4-3 shows corrosion around the seam sealed by the head gasket on a typical engine.

This is in its early stages, but head-gasket failure is not far off, and this should be attended to soon.

Corrosion is most commonly associated with electrical problems and can spawn a variety of symptoms so, again, it's clearly one of the first things you should look for.

Figure 4-4 highlights a common breeding ground for corrosion that could affect many circuits. In Figure 4-4, the junction box indicated by the arrow services the engine's charging system as well as the electrically activated choke. Any green build-up of corrosion or loose connections at this point could cause a lot of trouble.

Use your eyes all you can. For example, watch for signs of paint discoloration on your engine block. This is an indication of overheating.

Kinks in fuel lines or control cables or wiring that

Figure 4-2. *Checking that fuel is reaching the carburetor.*

Figure 4-3. *Head gasket beginning to leak—note corrosion at the joint.*

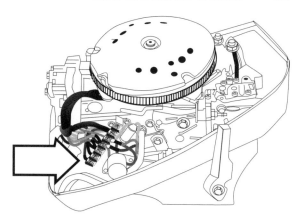

Figure 4-4. *Checking for corrosion at a typical electrical junction block.*

has a frayed outer sheathing should be obvious clues to potential problems. Figure 4-5 shows an engine throttle cable with a frayed outer sheath. Water is going to seep into the cable housing, causing hidden corrosion

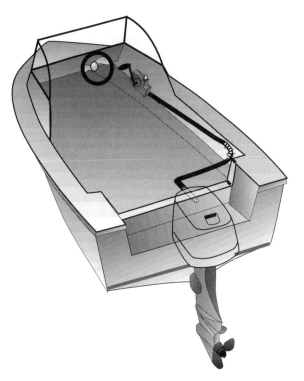

Figure 4-5. *Engine control cable showing frayed outer cover.*

and, ultimately, cable binding that will affect throttle operation. This particular cable should be replaced.

And don't forget your sense of smell. It, too, can lead you to the source of problems on board. If you smell fuel, for instance, you could be on the track of a potentially dangerous leak that needs immediate attention. There are certain other odors that point to problems as well. A foul, rotten-egg smell near your battery can indicate extreme overcharging, and must be followed up with complete checks of the engine's charging system and the battery's condition.

You probably already know the often-frightening smell of overheated electrical wiring and components. It indicates a problem that must be traced quickly, before serious damage results.

Oil leaking from an oil-injection system will collect on the hot engine block and emit its own distinct foul smell and probably create some smoke, too, depending on the severity of the leak. Again, immediate attention is needed.

Lastly there's your sense of touch. Use it to find loosely mounted engine components such as starters, regulators, fuel pumps, and the like, before they fall off. Steering that binds or feels too loose must be attended to. Wiring that feels warm to the touch as the circuit is activated is a sign of excessive resistance in the wiring and the real danger of fire. The problem could simply be a loose connection, or possibly a wire cable that's undersized for the electrical load it's carrying. A trim tab that feels loose in its mount can cause steering problems and may need adjustment.

The bottom line here is that to be a good troubleshooter you need more than just technical knowledge. Troubleshooting is a craft that must be practiced. You must develop a keen sense for what sounds, feels, looks, and smells right, and use these senses to help you home in on the area of trouble.

A Troubleshooting Plan of Attack

To develop a quick plan of attack, you need to know what problems outboard engines are most prone to. Here's a list of the systems in order of frequency of failure:

- Fuel system.
- Oiling system.

- Cooling system.
- Electrical system.
- Boat or engine-mounting problems.

Details for solving problems in each of these general categories can be found in the appropriate chapter of this book.

Ten Categories of Trouble. Common symptoms of trouble can be placed in 10 basic categories:

1. The engine will not start.
2. The engine runs irregularly or stalls.
3. The engine idles unevenly.
4. Engine speed will not increase above idle.
5. The engine overheats.
6. The engine speed is higher than normal.
7. The engine speed is lower than normal.
8. Boat speed is less than normal.
9. Boat pulls or steers to one side or the other.
10. The engine is emitting excessive blue smoke.

Once you establish which of these symptoms describes your problem, consult the following step-by-step troubleshooting chart. Keep in mind the basic needs of an engine that I drilled into you in Chapter One, and realize that many of the following symptoms are the direct result of those needs not being met.

Note that I've listed the probable causes of trouble in the order of most frequent occurrence—assuming that normal engine maintenance has been performed.

Symptoms and Probable Causes

Engine Will Not Start

1. Fuel tank empty.
2. Fuel supply hose incorrectly attached.
3. Fuel supply hose crushed or kinked.
4. Faulty fuel pump.
5. Fuel contaminated or old and stale.
6. Not following correct starting procedure.
7. Defective or fouled spark plug(s).
8. Incorrect spark plugs.
9. Plug wires not pushed in place tightly.
10. Emergency shut-off not de-activated.
11. Battery undercharged.
12. Ignition wiring or connections faulty.
13. Bad ignition coil.

14. Ignition switch defective.
15. Faulty CDI ignition system component.
16. Starter motor defective.

Engine Runs Irregularly or Stalls

1. Fuel tank empty.
2. Fuel supply hose incorrectly installed.
3. Fuel tank vent closed or restricted.
4. Fuel hose crushed or kinked.
5. Fuel filter plugged.
6. Fuel contaminated or old and stale.
7. Incorrect starting procedure.
8. Specified engine oil has not been used.
9. Spark plug(s) fouled or defective.
10. Incorrect spark plug.
11. Incorrect spark-plug gap.
12. Thermostat clogged or faulty.

Rough Idle

1. Fuel hose crushed or kinked.
2. Fuel filter clogged.
3. Fuel contaminated or old and stale.
4. Fouled or defective spark plug(s).
5. Incorrect spark plug.
6. Incorrect plug gap.
7. Faulty ignition to one or more cylinder(s).

Engine Speed Will Not Increase

1. Fuel supply hose incorrectly connected.
2. Fuel hose crushed or kinked.
3. Fuel filter clogged.
4. Engine oil level low.
5. Spark plug(s) fouled or defective.
6. Propeller has incorrect pitch or diameter.
7. Boat is overloaded.

Engine Overheats

1. Clogged water passages.
2. Boat overloaded.
3. Engine oil level is low.
4. Incorrect engine oil.

5. Oil is old, stale, or contaminated.
6. Oil pump is malfunctioning.
7. Faulty water pump.
8. Wrong heat-range spark plug.
9. Thermostat clogged or defective.

Engine Speed Higher than Normal

1. Propeller cavitation.
2. Damaged propeller.
3. Engine trim angle incorrect.
4. Propeller pitch or diameter incorrect.
5. Transom too high.

Engine Speed Lower than Normal

1. Fuel hose crushed or kinked.
2. Fuel filter clogged.
3. Fuel contaminated, or old and stale.
4. Spark plug(s) fouled or defective.
5. Incorrect spark plug.
6. Spark-plug gap incorrect.
7. Badly fouled propeller.
8. Propeller pitch or diameter incorrect.

Boat Speed Low

1. Propeller cavitation.
2. Propeller damaged.
3. Incorrect trim angle.
4. Boat is overloaded.
5. Bottom severely fouled with sea growth.
6. Incorrect propeller pitch or diameter.
7. Transom too low.
8. Transom too high.

Steering Pulls to One Side

1. Boat loaded unevenly.
2. Engine-mounted trim tab out of adjustment.

Excessive Blue Smoke

1. Incorrect fuel/oil mix.
2. Oil-injection system faulty.

Chapter 5

Isolating Ignition System Problems

When your engine begins to skip and misfire, or won't start at all, one of its basic needs is not being met. It may be a fault in the ignition system. To help in the process of isolating ignition system problems, it's helpful to know exactly what the ignition system must do on your engine.

Manufacturers have devised slightly different methods to achieve the same goal, which is to create an electrical spark capable of blasting its way through a dense, compressed fog of fuel, oil, and air with enough heat to set it alight.

This spark must be delivered to the correct cylinder at the correct time, and with equal intensity for all cylinders. In addition, as the engine speed changes, so must the timing. On today's engines, these tasks are undertaken by a combination of solid state devices, electronic wizardry, and a mechanical linkage to advance the ignition timing. Figure 5-1 shows a typical outboard engine ignition system with all the key components named.

On outboard ignition systems, some of the primary operating components are located under the flywheel, so, as with some of the other procedures mentioned in this book, you may need the services of a trained mechanic with the correct puller tool to reach these parts. Also, test procedures in workshop manuals call for special equipment such as Stevens or Merc-O-Tronic

ignition system testers. This equipment is quite expensive, and really has no place in your tool kit unless you do this sort of work daily. So there are a few things you'll have to leave to the experts. But this chapter will show you how to figure out the most common ignition problems with the use of simple tools, and a multimeter that you really should have in your tool collection anyway.

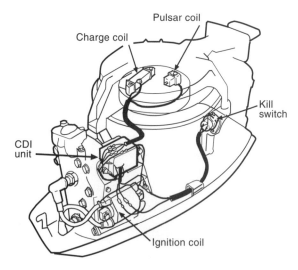

Figure 5-1. *Outboard engine capacitive discharge ignition system.*

If your engine was built after about 1975, it most likely has some variation of a capacitive discharge (CD) ignition system. This system "charges up" a capacitor or condenser, a simple device capable of storing an electric charge and discharging it very rapidly. The charge then goes to the appropriate ignition coil. Different manufacturers use various names to describe the CD components they use, but they're all quite similar.

Ignition Components, and What They Do

Here's a detailed description of the typical components of a modern ignition system, and their functions:

The engine's **flywheel** contains magnets carefully positioned to create an electric current as they rotate past specially designed coils of wire. Current is created by magnetic induction. Simply put, that means that a magnet moving rapidly near a conductor will induce electrical flow within the conductor.

Conversely, a wire that moves rapidly through a magnetic field will also generate electrical flow. This principle governs the working of electric motors, alternators, and generators.

One of the coils under your flywheel is called a **charge coil.** As the flywheel magnets spin past this coil, they generate in it a fairly high-voltage alternating current that travels to your system's **"module,"** often called the **power pack** or **CDI unit** (see below). This voltage will be in the region of 200 volts AC.

The other ignition system coil(s) found under the flywheel are called the **sensor coils** (OMC), **pulsar coils** (Yamaha), or **trigger coils** (Mercury). They send an electrical signal to the ignition module to tell it which cylinder to work with at the correct time.

The **CDI unit** is the brains of the system and serves several functions. First, it converts the alternating current (AC) from the charge coil into usable direct current (DC). Next it stores the current in the built-in **capacitor** mentioned earlier. The module also interprets the timing signal from the trigger coil. This changes constantly with engine speed, and the change is brought about by moving the trigger coil's position relative to the flywheel magnets. The coil's movement is controlled by a device called a **timing plate**, to which both the charge coil and trigger coils are mounted. The timing plate moves in response to changes in the carburetor throttle opening, to which it is linked mechanically. The CDI unit also controls the discharge of the capacitor and sends this voltage to the "primary" winding of the **ignition coil** for the correct cylinder.

Also (depending on the system) the module may incorporate electronic circuits that limit engine speed and prevent over-revving. Some modules even have a circuit that reduces engine speed if the engine begins to run too hot for any reason. Larger engines often have an **automatic ignition advance** for initial start-up and for when the engine is running at temperatures of less than approximately 100°F.

Manufacturers commonly use one power pack, or module, for each bank of cylinders on V-type powerheads. One module will control the odd-numbered cylinders and the other will service the even-numbered cylinders.

As you saw above, the voltage from the module goes to the primary winding of the **ignition coil,** or **high-tension coil**. You may know this type of coil as a step-up transformer. Here, the voltage is stepped up to between 15,000 and 40,000 volts. That's the kind of voltage needed to jump the air gap we talked about before, and ignite the air/fuel mixture in the cylinder. Your high-tension ignition coil has two "sides," the primary and the secondary. It is really two coil assemblies combined into one neat, compact case.

Figure 5-2 shows the internal construction of a typical ignition coil, with its primary and secondary windings. It also uses the principle of magnetic induction, with the magnetism generated by the primary (lower voltage) winding creating a magnetic field around the secondary winding, which you will notice has many more windings than the primary coil. The ignition module controls the rapid turning on and off of electrical flow in the primary winding, thereby turning this magnetic field on and off. The effect of this is the same as described earlier. The rapid movement of this magnetic field past the secondary windings induces electrical current flow. The greater the number of turns of wire in the secondary winding, the higher the voltage produced.

As this secondary voltage leaves the center tower of the ignition coil, it travels along the **spark-plug wire**, which is heavily insulated and designed to carry this high voltage.

If all is well, the high voltage will jump the gap in

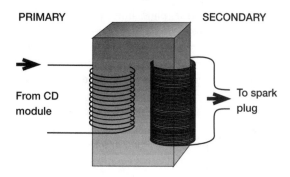

PRIMARY   SECONDARY

From CD module

To spark plug

Figure 5-2. *High-tension coil—internal construction.*

the **spark plug** between the center electrode and the ground electrode. On larger engines with **surface-gap plugs,** the high-voltage current will jump from the center electrode to the side of the plug assembly itself, completing a circuit to "ground"—the engine block the plug is threaded into.

Last, but certainly not least, is the **stop control**. You need a means to shut your engine off, and a good way is to stop the spark plugs working. Depending on your engine, this may be accomplished by a simple stop button, or a key switch on larger engines, that disables the whole ignition system. On newer engines,

you'll find an **emergency stop button** with an **overboard clip and lanyard attachment.** This system is wired directly to your system's ignition module (power pack). It functions by creating a momentary short-circuit inside the CDI power pack, grounding the current intended for the high-tension coils and thus shutting off the ignition long enough to stop the engine. Faulty stop circuits are frequently the cause of a no-spark condition; test procedures for this circuit are outlined later in this chapter on page 39.

Ignition Tests

As with any electrical circuit testing, the first step should be to look for the obvious. Whenever a problem develops with any engine or system that has been regularly maintained, troubles that crop up are almost always due to some minor oversight, and easily solved.

- Check all the wiring hook-ups for loose connections.
- Look for signs of corrosion on terminals and at connectors.
- Check for any broken or frayed wires.
- Make certain the problem is not something as silly as a blown fuse.

Figure 5-3. *A surface-gap spark plug (left) and a conventional plug.*

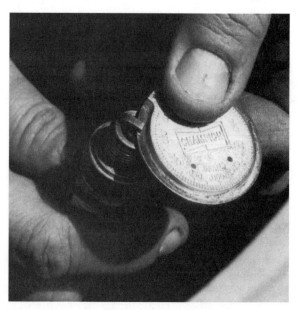

Figure 5-4. *Using a spark plug gapping tool.*

Any of these things can be the cause of ignition problems—but they can be fixed quickly with basic tools.

Testing for Spark

The next step in checking out your ignition system is to verify that you're getting spark to each cylinder. When you're doing this it's extremely important that you check for fuel leaks. Make certain all fuel-line fittings and connections are secure.

Incidentally, if you're working in bright daylight, it's a good idea to create some shade near the plug wire you're checking. It's very difficult to see a spark in sunlight.

You'll do best with an inexpensive spark tester such as the one shown in Figure 5-5.

This very useful unit is marketed by Snap-On Tools, and costs only about seven or eight dollars. The unit shown has been modified for increased safety in marine use. The idea is to enclose the spark so that it becomes "ignition protected." To do this, take a piece of clear ⅝-inch freshwater hose and cut off a 2-inch length. Slice this piece lengthwise for its entire length. Take some "super glue" and lay a bead along the edge of the open face on the standard spark tester. Then, spread the plastic hose piece open and lay it carefully over the open face of the tool. Press the edges onto the glue bead. The glue will bond the hose to the tester and effectively seal the contacts of the tool in the fully enclosed cylinder you have just created. You'll still be able to see the spark jump inside the cylinder through the clear hose, but you won't have to worry about the spark biting you as you hold the tool.

To use the tool, carefully remove the plug wire from the spark plug you wish to test, and use a twisting, pulling motion on the plug's wire boot only. Never pull on the wire itself, as you may damage the connection inside the boot where the wire attaches to its end connector.

Insert the heavy brass terminal end of the tool into the plug wire end, making sure it fits snugly into the boot. Now take the wire lead from the spark tester and attach the clip to a good ground point on the engine. Make sure the ground connection is good, and remember that paint acts as an insulator. You may have to scrape a little away to get a good connection. Next, adjust the knurled knob on the tool to a gap of about ⅜ inch or ⁷⁄₁₆ inch between the two pointed contacts inside the cylinder.

Figure 5-6 shows the tool hooked up properly and ready to go. Hold the tool so you can see inside the cylinder, and crank the engine over. You should see a

Figure 5-6. *The Snap-On tester in place and ready to use.*

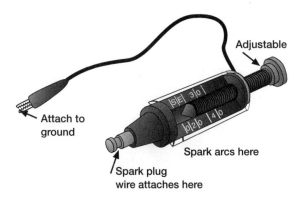

Figure 5-5. *A Snap-On spark tester.*

bright blue spark jumping between the two contact points. If you do, then total ignition output is satisfactory. If you don't, or if the spark is yellow, further investigation will be needed.

If your engine is skipping or misfiring, you should check all of the plug wires this way to be certain that each secondary coil is sending spark through its respective plug wire to the plug.

The beauty of this particular tool over others is that the air gap between the two contacts is adjustable. This is important because some manufacturers give an air-gap specification in their manuals. The wider the air gap a spark will jump, the higher the total ignition system output. So, by comparing the maximum gap jump for each ignition coil, you can isolate a weak or faulty coil.

By the way, be careful not to mix the plug wires up when you perform this test; each wire is timed to a specific cylinder. Make sure the emergency stop button and clip are set correctly if your engine is so equipped. (It's amazing how easy it is to forget this simple device.) Check for spark again. If spark is still not evident, further investigation will be needed.

Testing the Plugs

Unfortunately, there's no guarantee that if you get an appropriately hefty electrical current to the spark plugs, they'll fire. They may simply be worn out. And many other things can cause a plug in your engine not to fire.

For example, too much oil in the fuel is a primary cause of spark-plug failure. So is the use of a plug with an incorrect heat range. Problems with the fuel system also can result in spark-plug failure.

Now, if you've been conscientious and serviced your engine regularly as described in Chapter Three, worn-out plugs shouldn't be a consideration. What does that leave? A visual check of the plugs, and verification that the plug itself can actually fire.

Remove the plug, using the appropriate spark-plug socket or the plug removal tool supplied in the tool kit for your engine, and look it over. Is it soaked with a black fuel/oil mixture? Are the center and ground electrodes intact?

If the plug's center and ground electrodes are okay, and the plug is gapped correctly, check the number on

the plug and compare it with the manufacturer's recommendations. It may be the wrong heat range for the engine.

If all of these things check out okay, then insert the plug into its correct plug wire boot, and wedge the plug into a spot on the side of your engine as shown in Figure 5-7, being sure that the metal case of the plug is grounded.

Crank the engine over. If you see a spark jumping from the center electrode to the edge of the plug on a surface-gap plug, or to the ground electrode on a standard unit, and it's blue in color, then it's okay and should fire in the cylinder. If no spark is evident, or it's weak and yellow, and you are certain (from your previous spark intensity check) that adequate current is getting to the plug, then the plug must be replaced. If it's a standard plug, make sure to check the gap before

Figure 5-7. *Testing a spark plug on the engine block.*

installing the new plug, as shown in Figure 5-4. Surface-gap plugs require no adjustment.

When you've had a bit of experience, you'll find that your spark plugs are valuable diagnostic tools. Whenever you remove your plugs, keep them in order according to the cylinders they came from and check each plug over carefully, looking for any cracks in the ceramic body or insulator, black oily build-up, or discoloration.

A spark plug that is burning correctly will show a light brown "fluffy" coloration on the center electrode's ceramic insulator, and a fluffy black coloration on the metal base, with the exception of the ground electrode itself, which will show a light gray/brown color.

One last thing regarding spark plugs, and that is to be careful not to over-torque them (screw them in too tightly) when replacing them. It's a good idea to put a light coating of white grease on the threads before screwing them back into the cylinder head. Screw them in by hand until the sealing washer seats, and then use your special plug tool or socket and ratchet to tighten them an additional quarter to half a turn. Any more may damage the plug threads in the cylinder head.

Ignition Problems— Tests and Procedures

If you have performed the spark checks described above, and determined that you have no spark at any of the cylinders, or spark at some and not others, then further investigation is needed.

The following checklist is designed to organize your search through the ignition system, and the tests that follow will help you to pinpoint the source of the problem. Remember, these tests should be performed by using this book *and* the manual for your particular engine.

Each manufacturer uses different wire-color codes, and slightly different test procedures for their respective systems, but by following this guide you should be able to trace through your system and isolate any CD ignition system problems, in the rare instance that they occur.

One last reminder: These test sequences assume that you have already eliminated the possibility of a fuel-related or compression-related problem.

Ignition Problem Checklist

1. Begin by checking to see if your engine is equipped with a fuse for the ignition system. If it is, check the fuse, and replace it if needed.
2. Check the plug wires.
3. Test the ignition coils.
4. Test the outputs of the charge coil, sensor coil, and the ignition module; and test the integrity of the whole circuit. Use a multimeter and a Mercury DVA tester (part number 91-89045).
5. Test all engine stop circuits.
6. Test the mercury tilt switch if your engine is equipped with one.

Detailed procedures follow for each of these checks.

Testing Spark-Plug Wires

Here's a nice easy job. If you have already used the spark tester and seen a spark at the plug end of the wire, then you know the wire is conducting electricity to the plug. But that's not all the wire has to do. It also has to insulate this high-voltage electricity under all engine operating conditions. It has to conduct electricity on a vibrating engine when your boat is underway, and stop the electricity leaking out to the many metal components all around it, which would ground it.

So start with a visual inspection of the wire and the wire ends inside the protective boots. Look for any sign of cracking, spots where the insulating material has been worn away due to chafing with some part of your engine, and any sign of green corrosion on the metal clips that lock the wire end to the coil and spark plug. If corrosion is evident, slide the wire boot back onto the wire and carefully clean the metal connector with a wire brush until the metal is bright and shiny. If the wire is chafed or cracked, replace it.

For further checks, you'll need your multimeter. Set the meter on the low ohms scale and insert the meter probes into the wire as shown in Figure 5-8. The meter should read near zero ohms. Next, hold the meter probes in place and bend and flex the wire while you watch the meter carefully. If the meter fluctuates, there is a break in the wire inside the insulation. Replace the wire. When reinstalling wires, make sure to use the wire hold-downs found on many engines.

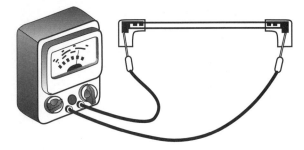

Figure 5-8. *Using the ohmmeter to test a plug wire.*

These hold-downs are there to keep the wire from coming in contact with moving parts of the engine that may cause chafe and ultimately wire failure. Also, all manufacturers recommend applying a light coating of non-conductive waterproof grease on the ribbed ceramic insulator and metal connector of the spark plug and coil connector before re-installing the plug wire. This grease will help the boot to seal out moisture that would eventually corrode the metal connector end of the plug wire.

Testing High-Tension Coils

A technician in a repair shop will normally use one of the system testers specially designed to work with outboard engines. These units are quite expensive and don't need to be a part of your tool collection. This means you won't be able to perform some of the more advanced ignition system tests. But if you have a multimeter, a spray bottle filled with fresh water, and the spark tester already mentioned, you'll be well equipped to track down most ignition faults. At the very least, you'll be able to point the professional mechanic in the right direction, saving yourself expensive labor charges.

As we've already seen, your ignition coil is really two coils combined into one unit. It consists of two sets of wire windings, a primary winding and a secondary winding. The trick is to identify which external wires and connections go to which coil inside the insulated case. To find out, you'll need the wiring diagram and workshop manual for your engine. Refer to the wiring diagram and check the resistance of each

of the coils with your multimeter's ohmmeter. If electrical continuity and normal resistance is shown with these tests, you can be reasonably certain your coils are okay. If you discover excessive resistance, or if the meter indicates an open circuit in the coil, the coil must be replaced.

Figure 5-9 shows these tests being performed on a typical outboard engine high-tension coil. But please remember that it's absolutely vital to identify the wires correctly so you can ascertain their relative resistance values.

Incidentally, whenever you remove an ignition coil from your engine, be extremely careful to note the location of any insulating washers located under the coils or their hold-down bolts. If you misplace this insulation it's likely that even a perfectly good coil won't work.

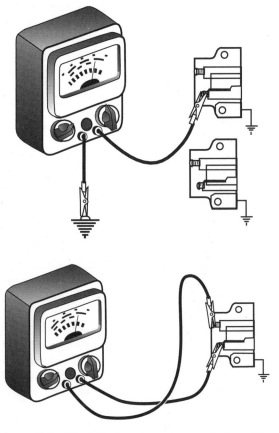

Figure 5-9. *(Top) Testing the primary winding. (Bottom) Testing the secondary winding.*

Another simple test for this part of your ignition system is to spray fresh water over the ignition coils, plug wires, and spark plugs while the engine's running. Do this in the shade, or at dusk. Any problems will immediately show as sparks, jumping from the poorly insulated wire or connection. The faulty component will have to be replaced.

Testing Charge and Sensor Coils and Ignition Module

For these tests you will again need your engine's workshop manual. Remember, your charge coil and sensor coil lie under the flywheel, and you can't see them unless you remove it. Unfortunately, flywheel removal goes beyond routine testing, and is not within the scope of this book, but there are still several useful tests you can perform. For example, you can test the charge coils and sensor coils for continuity and a possible short to ground. You can also test their voltage output using the Mercury DVA tester in conjunction with your multimeter.

Just like your high-tension coil, these coils consist of a tightly wound length of wire, insulated from the ground in most cases. In all cases, the charge coil will have a greater designed resistance than the sensor coil. The reason for this is that the charge coil must generate higher voltage than the sensor coils. This means the length of wire in the coil will be much longer, and therefore have more inherent resistance.

The wiring harness for these coils is always secured to the movable timing plate under the flywheel and usually exits from under this assembly on the starboard side (right side, looking toward the bow of the boat) of the engine powerhead. Once you have located the harness and found all the wires that come through it, use the wiring diagram to identify the wires attached to the charge and sensor coils. These wires will often end up at a gang plug assembly for connection to your ignition module. Unplug this connection to continue testing.

Testing the Charge Coil. To test the charge coil, set your ohmmeter to the appropriate scale for the expected resistance as specified in your engine manual. Insert your meter's red and black test probes into the plug socket terminal that matches the correct color wire, and take the reading.

Charge coils generally have a resistance of 400 to 900 ohms. If the reading is more than specified, or indicates a break in the wiring (infinite reading), the charge coil is defective, and will have to be replaced.

Next, you must check for a short to ground. To perform this test, simply remove one of the meter's test leads from the plug assembly, switch your meter to its high ohms scale, and touch the free lead to the metal timing plate the harness is secured to. Any movement of the meter needle indicates a short to ground caused by frayed or melted insulation, or by a bad charge coil. In both cases the flywheel will have to be removed to fix the problem.

Testing the Sensor Coil. To test a sensor coil for continuity and a short to ground, follow the exact procedure given above for the charge-coil tests, only remember to adjust your meter for a much lower resistance reading, usually between 15 and 50 ohms.

For the short-to-ground test, the meter will be set on the same high scale as for the charge-coil short test. Remember to test all sensor coils in this manner if your engine is equipped with more than one.

Testing Coil Voltages. To test for voltage output from these coils you will need to use the DVA adapter as shown in Figure 5-11. This device will convert the AC voltage from your charge and sensor coils to a DC voltage your multimeter can read. The readings you

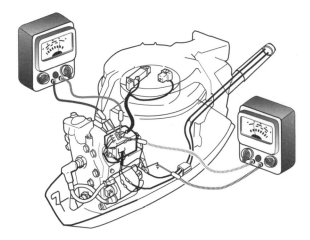

Figure 5-10. *Testing charge and sensor coils. Note the point at which the wiring harness exits from under the flywheel, and the timing-plate assembly.*

Figure 5-11. *Testing voltage output with the DVA tester.*

get here will not only test the performance of these coils but also verify that the magnets under your flywheel still have sufficient magnetism. Voltage output is directly proportional to the cranking speed of the engine and the strength of these magnets.

To test output, simply plug the red lead from the tester into the DC voltage socket on your multimeter and the black lead from the tester into the ground or negative socket on your meter. Next, plug the red and black leads from your meter into the corresponding sockets on the DVA tester. You're ready to take a voltage reading now.

Charge-Coil Test.   To test the charge-coil output you should set your voltmeter to a scale that will read as much as about 400 volts. Typical readings at cranking speed for charge coils are between 150 and 275

volts. You must check the workshop manual for your engine to get the exact specification for this.

Next, plug the meter leads into the socket or connect to the leads coming from the charge coil. Again, your manual will help you identify these two wires. Next crank the engine over, or use the pull cord and take a reading from your meter. If the reading you get is within specifications, your charge coil has tested fully okay and is not the source of any ignition problems.

Sensor-Coil Test.   Next test the sensor coil following the same procedure as for the charge coil, only for this coil you must switch to a low volt reading—20 volts or less. Typical sensor-coil output readings will be between 1.2 and 9 volts at cranking speed. Again, verify the specification in your engine's manual. Make sure to check all the sensor coils if your engine is equipped with more than one.

Ignition-Module Test.   Next, you can test the ignition module's output to each of the high-tension coils using the meter and DVA adapter. For this test it's important to be sure the ground wire for your ignition module is secure, as damage to the module could occur if it is not.

Once you've located this ground wire you can attach to it the black lead from your multimeter/DVA combination. Also, it's a good idea to use your wiring diagram to locate the stop-circuit ground lead for your ignition module. Disconnect it from the stop circuit. This will isolate the ignition module from that circuit, and eliminate the possibility of a defect in the stop circuit leading you to misdiagnose your ignition module as faulty.

Next, switch your meter to a scale capable of reading as much as about 400 volts. Locate the high-tension coil primary feed wire (the wire that connects from the ignition module to the coil), attach your meter's red lead to the terminal point at the high-tension coil where this wire is attached, and crank over the engine. Your reading here, which will be somewhere between 150 and 350 volts, is the output voltage from the capacitor inside the ignition module. Match your reading to factory specifications for your engine. Perform this test for each ignition module output lead on your engine. You readings should be approximately the same for each lead on your module. If you discover a lead with no output, or a considerably lower output (check your engine's tolerance in the workshop manual), the ignition module is defective and must be replaced.

Under-the-Flywheel Systems. In some of the latest CD ignition systems, the ignition module is *under* the flywheel, and the sensor coils have been integrated with the module pack. In this case, you won't be able to touch the charge coil wiring, and you won't find any reference to sensor-coil testing in your workshop manual. The flywheel must be removed to service these components on this type of system. If your engine is like this, and your tests on the plugs, secondary wiring, and high-tension coils lead you to this point, you will need the services of your dealer.

I should emphasize that problems with charge coils, sensor coils, and the permanent magnets under the flywheel are extremely rare. You shouldn't ever have to deal with them on your engine. The only thing that classically causes early failure of these components is lack of early attention when an engine has been accidentally submerged in salt water. This saltwater exposure induces excessive corrosion, resulting in resistance to the electrical flow and premature failure. The correct procedures for handling a saltwater dunking are outlined in Chapter 10.

Some Additional Checks

Let's pause here for a moment before we tackle the final tests of the ignition system. At this stage, you know how to verify your system's spark output with a seven-dollar tester. You know how to remove spark plugs, check them, and replace them. You know how to check the plug wires and the high-tension coils. You should also be able to check your charge and sensor coils with the help of your workshop manual. So what's left, you ask? What else could possibly cause ignition trouble? Well, there are a few things you might have to investigate one day. Your engine's stop circuit is one of them. And then there's timing. Finally, your ignition module may have some additional functions you'll need to look at. Let's take one thing at a time:

Testing Your Stop Switch. Your engine may have a remote key switch to turn the ignition on and off. Or, if it's a smaller engine, it may have a simple stop button mounted directly on the engine or steering tiller. In either case, the tool of choice for testing the circuit will be your ohmmeter. In addition, of course, you'll need the wiring diagram for your engine.

If you don't have a remote-control ignition switch, you'll need to begin your search under the engine cowl at the point where the wiring and cable controls exit the steering tiller assembly. One lead goes to a good engine ground, and the other goes to the ignition module. Verify that you have the correct wires by checking your engine-wiring diagram.

Install the emergency stop clip if your engine is so equipped. Your engine should now be in the run mode. Now find a good ground point on your engine and with your meter's black lead attached to ground, install the red lead in the plug assembly or attach it to the previously identified wire coming from the stop button.

Your meter should give you a high (infinity) reading indicating an open circuit if all is well. Any reading showing continuity indicates the switch is defective, or the wire coming from the switch is shorted to ground somewhere inside your tiller handle. In either case, you'll have to replace the assembly.

If all appears okay to this point, push the stop button in and check your meter; it should show a low reading, indicating continuity. Finally, if equipped, pull the clip out and observe your meter reading; the meter should show a low reading again. If pushing the stop button or pulling the emergency clip does not give the desired low ohmmeter reading, the assembly must be replaced. Figure 5-12 shows a typical meter hookup for these tests.

On larger engines, you will still be checking switch function and for short circuits to ground. In this case you'll just have a little more distance to cover—the distance between your engine's powerhead and the key switch itself. Again, you will use your ohmmeter and need your engine's wiring diagram.

For these tests you will need to positively identify *all* the terminal connections on the back of your key switch. To get to the switch, you may have to unfasten your assembly from the boat and remove the back cover of the control unit.

Some good manuals give a detailed picture of the plug assembly coming from the back of this switch, and identify all the terminal connections. In that case, if you can reach the plug, you won't have to remove the remote-control assembly to perform these tests.

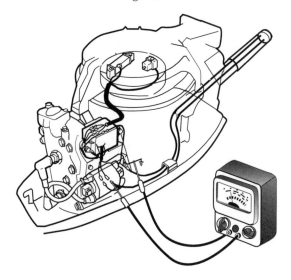

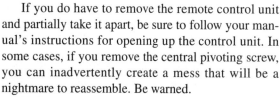

Figure 5-12. *Testing the stop circuit.*

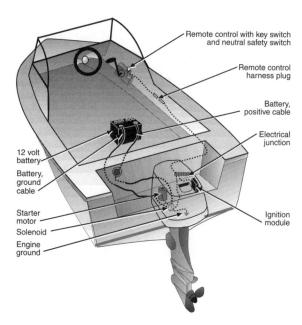

Figure 5-13. *Remote ignition switch installation.*

If you do have to remove the remote control unit and partially take it apart, be sure to follow your manual's instructions for opening up the control unit. In some cases, if you remove the central pivoting screw, you can inadvertently create a mess that will be a nightmare to reassemble. Be warned.

If the remote ignition switch is separate from the shift control, you shouldn't have a problem. Simply look for the back of the switch. You can usually get to it without removing the switch from the panel.

See your wiring diagram to identify the wire coming from the back of the ignition switch to the ground shut-off at the power pack. As with the smaller engines, this wire will usually terminate at a gang plug under the engine cowl in the harness going to the power pack. Once you're absolutely positive about its identity, disconnect the plug or connection to the module. Now you're ready for your ohmmeter tests. Start at the engine end.

First, connect the red test lead from your ohmmeter to the ignition-switch terminal that goes to the module. Connect your black test lead to a good engine ground. With the ignition key in the "on" position, your meter should give a high reading, infinity on the scale.

If your meter shows a complete circuit, indicated by a near 0 resistance reading, you must disconnect

this same wire from the back of the ignition switch and check the meter reading again. If the meter now reads infinity, the ignition switch itself is faulty and must be replaced. If the meter indicates a complete circuit to ground, shown by little or no resistance on the gauge, then the wire that connects the ignition switch to the engine is shorted to ground and must be repaired.

If all of these readings check out okay, turn the key switch to the "off" position and check your meter. You should have a low resistance, reading near 0 ohms. If your meter still gives a reading of infinity, then you must check that the terminal and wire indicated by your engine wiring diagram as ground for the key switch are connected and in good condition. If they are, then you may have a break (open circuit) in the wire leading from the switch to the terminal on the engine. You'll have to check the entire length of this wire and either install a new one or splice the break. Figure 5-13 shows a typical wiring diagram for a remote-key installation, with the typical test points shown, and the possibly faulty wires indicated.

If, after performing all of these tests to your engine's stop circuit(s) you still have a problem with your engine not shutting down with either the key switch or the stop button, then the only thing left in the circuit that could cause this fault is the ignition module itself. Unfortunately, it's a solid-state, completely sealed device, and you can't repair it in the field. You'll have to replace it.

Testing a Mercury (Tilt) Stop Switch. Some midsize and larger outboards have a switch located in the trim/mounting bracket assembly. It's designed to cut out the ignition if the engine is trimmed too much and fails to pick up cooling water. Figure 5-14 shows this switch on a 70-hp Mercury outboard.

To test the tilt switch, remove the mounting screw that secures it to the engine. Disconnect the remaining lead coming from the switch. Now set your ohmmeter to the low ohms scale and hook it to the two switch leads. It doesn't matter which lead goes where.

Position the switch in your hand as it would nor-

mally be on the engine in the trim-down position. Observe the meter. It should read no continuity or infinity. Next, tilt the switch in your hand and tap its high end with a finger. The meter should now indicate continuity through the switch. If your test readings show anything else, replace the mercury switch.

Final Checks and Ignition Timing

I don't want to depress you, but it's possible to do a thorough test of all the ignition components we've mentioned, have everything check out okay electrically, and still not have a spark. Or, you may have a strong spark in an engine that backfires when you try to start it, or misfires at high speed. Your ignition system could still be the culprit. Before condemning the ignition module for either of these faults, let's verify a few facts.

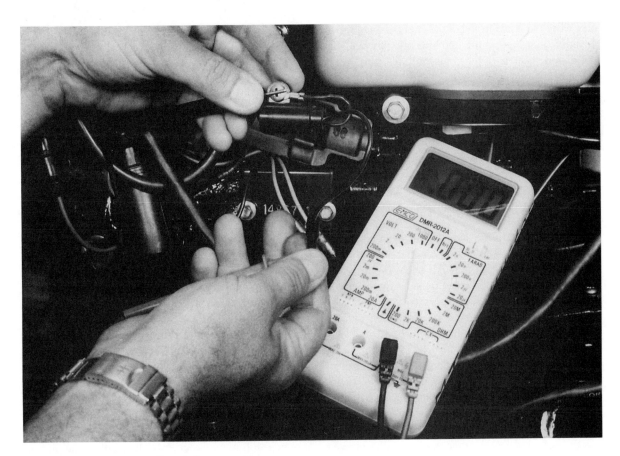

Figure 5-14. *A mercury tilt switch.*

First, you must be *absolutely certain* that all wires are hooked up correctly. It's all too easy to cross plug wires or switch primary feed wires going to the high-tension coils, so that the ignition module sends its signal to the wrong coil. Double-check everything with the help of your engine-wiring diagram. Gang-plug connections are always "keyed" so they can only fit together one way, but on engines with individual terminal connections, it's easy to make a mistake.

Also, make sure that all high-tension leads go back into their proper hold-down clamp on the engine, to avoid the possibility of a "crossfire" between cylinders.

Very rarely, the flywheel may be the culprit. Remember, it has carefully positioned magnets on its circumference. It's keyed to the engine's crankshaft so that these magnets pass by the appropriate charge or sensor coil at a carefully timed point in the engine's rotation.

On rare occasions (usually after the flywheel has been removed and improperly reinstalled) the flywheel may work loose on the end of the crankshaft and shear the positioning key. In this situation, the flywheel may "spin" independent of the crankshaft, altering the position of the magnets relative to the crankshaft position. The end result is an engine that is severely out of time.

To check for this, unplug the master plug to the ignition module to totally disable the ignition system. You don't want *any* risk of the engine starting with your hands on the flywheel. Next, grasp the flywheel firmly with both hands and feel for any movement from side to side or up and down, as shown in Figure 5-15.

Any evidence of movement indicates that the flywheel is loose on its mounting taper at the end of the crankshaft. The engine must be taken to an experienced mechanic. The flywheel must be removed, and the crankshaft and flywheel inspected, repaired, or replaced as needed. With any luck, you will need only a new key.

Checking the Timing.
If all the wiring is properly connected, and your flywheel is secure, then a timing check is in order. But you won't necessarily do it yourself. This is not a procedure for the inexperienced outboard engine mechanic to try.

First of all, there are different procedures for every outboard made. Secondly, for a precise job the ignition

Figure 5-15. *Checking the flywheel for looseness.*

timing pointer position must be verified, and that requires special tools the average boat owner won't have. Lastly, the timing should be checked not only at idle, but for maximum advance at high speed. This is best done in a special test tank, or with the aid of a dynamometer specially designed for outboard engines. The average boat owner *definitely* doesn't have these tools.

Don't give up hope, though. If you're well equipped and reasonably experienced, you can set the timing by following the instructions in your workshop manual. Look for the section titled "Engine Synchronization and Timing," or something similar. On small, single-carburetor engines, the procedure is not especially complicated, and the timing could be set even by someone with limited experience. Just follow the instructions carefully. On large engines, though, I wouldn't recommend that you try it. The variables are many, and go beyond the scope of this book.

To sum up the section on timing, here are the important facts again:

- Timing will rarely change unless someone inadvertently alters the carburetor linkage or adjustments; or
- The flywheel comes loose from the crankshaft; or
- The flywheel magnets work loose on the underside of the flywheel—fairly common on some engines; or
- The engine has many hours on it, and the timing plate under the flywheel is worn and suffers from excessive play.

So, if no one has tried to "adjust" your carburetor, and the flywheel isn't loose, it's highly unlikely that your ignition timing has changed. But, if you have any doubts based on all the information presented here, have a professional look at your timing.

If your engine has been quitting intermittently, or suddenly losing speed, again on an intermittent basis, there is still a remote possibility that your ignition module (CDI unit) is acting up.

CDI Unit Problems.

Unfortunately the ignition module is one component that may require you to rely on your dealer's expertise for some tests, particularly on midsize and large outboard engines. However, if your ignition problem was a lack of spark, and you have carefully performed *all* of the tests already outlined here, you can feel quite comfortable about purchasing a new module and installing it. That was your problem.

Other module-related problems are a little more difficult to pinpoint. Your module may incorporate a speed limiter. It could have a slow-down circuit designed to reduce revs if the engine overheats. If all your other tests point to the CD module (in anything other than a no-spark situation) inform your dealer of everything you have done, and rely on his advice about whether to replace the module. Remember, dealers will not accept returns on electrical components, so trial-and-error methods of testing can be expensive.

Optical Timing Systems.

If you own a midsize or large outboard engine made within the last several years, you may have an additional sub-system integrated into your CD ignition called *Optical Timing*. This is a very sophisticated system designed to electronically control timing advance and retard functions for easier starting and to control the timing with absolute precision.

Once again, unfortunately, this system requires a full arsenal of specialized test equipment and adapters to troubleshoot. If your engine is equipped with a system of this type, I can only advise you to consult your dealer for diagnosis if your problem search goes beyond checking fuses, corroded or loose connections, spark plugs, plug wires, and coils as described earlier in this chapter.

Summing It Up.

To sum up this chapter, just remember these important facts. In most cases, problems with ignition systems will be visible: a broken wire, a corroded connection, or simply a bad spark plug that should have been replaced long ago.

Because there are many engine manufacturers and many different ignition systems, you must use this book in conjunction with the right service manual for your engine.

When you follow the guidelines in this chapter, and the simplified test procedures, you'll be able to pinpoint all common ignition system problems (and some that aren't so common) and make the necessary repairs.

If your testing leads you to something that must be handled by the dealer, console yourself with the thought that you'll have saved a lot of labor dollars by doing the diagnostic tests yourself.

Chapter 6

The Charging and Starting Systems

If your engine is over about 6 hp and has an electric starter, it will have a charging system to keep your battery up to snuff. The battery will also run electrical accessories on your boat. When this charging and starting system fails, you'll need to pinpoint the troublesome component. This chapter will give you the insight you need to come up with an exact diagnosis every time.

Charging—The Key Components

Your charging system uses the principles of magnetic induction to produce electricity, just as your ignition system does. And like the CD ignition system, the charging system uses magnets positioned under your engine's flywheel. These magnets spin past a series of wire coils, and the result is an electrical charge that, with some modification, can be used to recharge your battery.

Figure 6-1 illustrates the entire system, showing the components of a typical charging system. The exact locations of the components on your engine may vary somewhat from those shown here, but no matter what kind of engine you have, all these bits and pieces will be on it somewhere.

The only thing that might differ from system to system, besides the actual wattage produced, is whether the final voltage is regulated or not. In general, the smaller engines do not bother with voltage regulation. This doesn't normally present any problems, but there are several considerations that apply to simple, non-regulated systems.

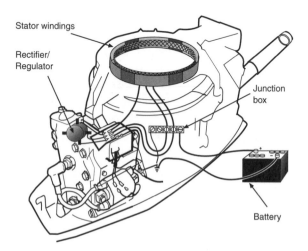

Figure 6-1. *The main components of the charging system.*

First, you should use only lead-acid batteries with removable cell tops. When a system has no voltage regulation, it will continue to charge the battery whenever the engine is running, whether the battery needs it or not.

If you don't have much electrical equipment on board to use up the generated electricity, it's quite possible to overcharge your battery and boil the electrolyte out. For this reason, you should frequently check the battery electrolyte level. Make sure the cells are not dry. The plates should be just covered with electrolyte.

Of course, if you have a regulated system, you don't have to worry about this problem, and you can use sealed, low-maintenance, or gel-celled batteries, as well as ordinary open-celled, lead-acid batteries.

How It All Works. To give you an idea of what's involved in creating and storing electrical energy from an outboard engine, here's a brief description of each component's function:

The **battery** stores electricity and acts as a "sponge" for the whole system. It mops up generated current until it's fully charged, and it releases energy on demand.

The **flywheel** holds the permanent magnets that create the moving magnetic field. If your engine has good spark, you can take it for granted that the magnets are in working order because the ignition and charging systems share the same magnets.

The **stator windings** are the stationary coils of wire the flywheel magnets rotate around. They produce the electrical charge. Simply put, the more windings in your stator, the greater the potential output in **amps** your charging system will have.

Next is the **rectifier**. It consists of a series of diodes, or electrical one-way valves. The rectifier overcomes one of the disadvantages of a current-generating system using permanent magnets and stator windings, which is that the current produced within the windings is alternating current (AC). You can't use AC to charge batteries. They accept only direct current (DC). So the rectifier is designed to convert AC current to a usable form of DC current simply called "rectified AC."

On midsize and large outboard engines, there may be a **voltage regulator,** either combined with the rectifier or standing alone. The regulator automatically reduces the output of generated current as the battery becomes fully charged.

Testing Your Battery

The heart of any charging system is the battery itself. That's why it's important for you to verify the battery's condition before making any assumptions about your engine's charging system.

First, you should check the battery's state of charge. An easy way to do this is to perform the "open-circuit voltage test." Always do this after the battery has been left idle for several hours. This allows the electrolyte and battery plate material to stabilize.

If you check a battery immediately after a long charging session, or right after adding distilled water to the cells, you'll get an extremely inaccurate reading. Also, remember to turn off all on-board electrical equipment when you're performing this test.

All you have to do is take a direct voltage reading with your multimeter from the battery's positive and negative terminals.

This test is best performed with a digital meter— you simply can't rely on your dashboard voltmeter. The accuracy required here is to within fractions of a volt, and dash-mounted analog meters simply won't do the job.

Here's the correlation between your open-circuit readings and the battery's state of charge:

Open-Circuit Voltage Test

Voltage Reading	Remaining Charge
12.6 or more	100 percent
12.4 to 12.6	75 to 100 percent
12.2 to 12.4	50 to 75 percent
12.0 to 12.2	25 to 50 percent
11.7 to 12.0	0 to 25 percent
11.7 or less	0

Note: If you're checking a "gel" type battery, you should expect these readings to be 0.2 volt to 1.0 volt higher.

Once you've determined the state of charge, and you've established that it's between 75 percent and 100 percent charged, an important additional test is the "battery capacity test, which will tell you about the battery's cranking and load-handling capability.

Battery Capacity Test. First, disable your engine's ignition system so the engine can't start. You can do this by disconnecting the main plug going into your CD ignition module if your engine has one. If not, disconnect all the engine's plug wires and use alligator-clip jumper leads to connect each plug wire end to a good engine ground. Be sure to do this for all the plug wires to avoid the possibility of damaging your ignition module. Or, if your engine is fairly new and has a safety-lanyard clip for a kill switch, simply remove the clip.

Once this step is complete, connect your voltmeter across your battery as for the open-circuit voltage test, and crank the engine over, either with the key switch or the starter button. Crank the engine for 15 seconds. At the end of that time, a battery voltage reading of 9.6 volts or more indicates that the battery has ample reserve capacity.

Battery Drain Test. The final check on a battery is to be certain that there is no unwanted drain on it. You should do this test whenever your battery starts losing its charge mysteriously. Before you start, though, be certain that the problem isn't something obvious. We've all left a VHF radio on for a week on low volume, or inadvertently left a baitwell pump running constantly. Those mysteries are easy to solve when you get over your embarrassment. Others need a bit of tracing.

To perform the test, turn off all electrical equipment on board. Remove the positive battery cable from its post on the battery. Connect the red lead of your voltmeter to the positive battery post, and the black lead to the battery cable clamp.

Any reading at all on your voltmeter indicates a draw from the battery that could drain it completely over a relatively short period of time if the engine isn't running. To correct this problem, you're going to have to disconnect each circuit individually until no voltage reading is indicated between the battery post and the cable connector. This will isolate the circuit giving the trouble.

But you're not out of the woods yet. Now you'll have to trace that troublesome circuit to find the cause of the constant draw. Depending upon the complexity of your boat, this could turn into a fairly complicated task. If you don't feel comfortable with troubleshooting problems in electrical circuits, call in an expert for help. At least you will have identified the general trouble area and exonerated your charging system.

Charging-System Problems and Possible Causes

So, what are the symptoms of charging-system problems, and the possible causes? The most obvious is a battery that continually goes dead. But that may be only the symptom of a failing battery that needs replacement. If you have tested the battery as described above, you will know if the battery itself is the problem.

Charging systems can develop problems that cause annoying results on board but have no effect on the battery. So don't jump to any conclusions until you've given the matter some deep thought with the help of the troubleshooting chart that follows. Remember, the components of this system are fairly expensive, and cannot be returned to the dealer, so guesswork can be costly.

Here's a series of common symptoms, and their probable causes. Work your way through it patiently until the culprit is exposed.

Charging-System Checklist

Symptom	Cause or Solution
Constantly adding water to battery, or rotten-egg odor from battery area.	Possible bad battery or, more likely, battery overcharging due to faulty regulator. Test and replace as needed.
Electrical "noise" from on-board radios, or loran signal problems; noise increasing with engine speed.	Faulty stator windings. Also could be caused by faulty grounding of radios or loran. Test stator windings for continuity or short to ground.
Lighting gets brighter as the engine speed increases.	If system is regulated, regulator is probably heavily overcharging. Test charge output and replace as needed. If unregulated, this can't be avoided. Just keep checking battery fluid level on a regular basis.
Battery weak, or going dead frequently.	1. Possible draw on battery with all systems off. Check for draw. 2. Undercharge condition. Test voltage regulator, replace as needed.

Symptom	Cause or Solution
	3. Charge and test battery condition. Replace as required. 4. Battery may be undersized for amount of electrical equipment on board. Analyze battery amp-hour capacity against average amperage draw on battery. 5. Charging system may have insufficient amperage output. May require optional high-output charging system.
Instrument panel voltmeter reading lower than normal.	Charging system faulty. Test entire system and replace the faulty component.

Verifying Charging-System Output.

How can you tell if your boat's charging system is functioning properly? A simple test is all that's required. If your boat has a built-in voltmeter, this task is even easier. It's called the "Three Step Voltage Test," and besides verifying the charging system's output, it will also isolate a problem with the voltage regulator, if you have one.

If your boat doesn't have a dashboard voltmeter, you'll need to use your multimeter set to the DC volts scale. Set the meter to 20 volts if it is not a self-scaling, automatic unit. All readings will be taken directly across the battery terminals. Your meter's black test lead will connect to the battery's negative terminal, and the red lead will connect to the battery's positive terminal.

If your boat does have a built-in voltmeter, then simply observe the gauge as you go through the sequence. Here are the three steps:

1. With all accessories on the boat turned off, take a direct reading at the battery to establish its **reference voltage.** If you have the built-in meter, simply turn the key to the on position. Write this number down, and be as accurate as possible, as fractions of volts are meaningful here.
2. Start your engine and run it at approximately 2,000 rpm. You should see an increase in voltage of between 1 volt and 3.5 volts. This reading is called the **unloaded voltage.**
   If the reading is more than 3.5 volts over the

reference voltage, your system is overcharging and the regulator is at fault. The regulator will have to be replaced.

If no change in the voltage reading is evident at the increased engine speed, then your charging system is not functioning. For non-regulated systems, the test ends here. The next step will be to determine the faulty component.

3. For regulated systems, the third and final step is to turn on as many accessories as possible with the engine maintaining 2,000 rpm. As these accessories are turned on, your voltage reading should begin to drop; but if the voltage regulator is functioning properly, you should get a reading of no less than about 0.5 volt greater than your **reference voltage**. This reading is referred to as the **regulated voltage**.

If your readings are less than 0.5 volt above the reference voltage, then your regulator is undercharging and should be replaced.

Testing Your AC Voltage Rectifier.

The rectifier is the charging-system component that most commonly gives trouble. These devices can be affected by overheating, voltage spikes, and (most frequently) by reversed polarity. Be warned: If you hook up your battery cables to the wrong terminal posts—positive to negative, and negative to positive—you can burn out your rectifier in a millisecond. In some cases, even running the engine with the battery disconnected can cause a voltage "spike" that will also destroy the rectifier. This isn't as much of a problem with some of the smaller engines, but do follow your owner's manual recommendations and always remember that it can happen.

Rectifiers consist of a series of diodes wired together and mounted in a "heat sink." This heat sink is the outer case of the unit, and its proper mounting to the engine is important to help conduct heat away from the rectifier. Diodes produce heat as they work, and the harder they're working the more heat they'll produce. Higher-output systems will also produce more heat. This need to get rid of heat by conduction is why you'll always find the rectifier or the combined rectifier/regulator securely mounted to the metal engine block, or in some cases, to the heavy metal casting of the carburetor air-box.

On some large engines, the rectifiers actually bolt right into the top of the engine block, with the back

48   *Outboard Engines*

side of the unit submerged in the engine's water jacket where it's constantly cooled by the circulating water. So again, anything that can cause this unit to overheat—such as improper mounting or even a restricted cooling system—can cause early failure of the rectifier and put a sudden stop to charging.

Testing the rectifier for damage is fairly simple, but you'll need the help of your workshop manual because the wiring colors and actual hook-up vary from one manufacturer to another. Some units can be tested in place, and others may have to be unbolted from the engine. Follow your workshop manual exactly, positively identifying each wire, and be sure to go through the complete test sequence.

As stated earlier, diodes are electronic devices that allow electrical flow only in one direction under normal circumstances. When diodes fail, they either allow voltage to flow in both directions, or they open the circuit completely, allowing no electricity to pass through them. So, by using the ohmmeter scale on your multimeter, your goal is to check for electrical continuity in one direction, and not in the other, for each diode in the rectifier.

Figures 6-2 and 6-3 show the ohmmeter being used to check the diodes of a typical rectifier as used on medium-sized Johnson and Evinrude engines.

Keep in mind that the rectifier on your engine may not look anything like this one, so be sure to verify the exact component on your engine.

By the way, before beginning any ohmmeter tests on your engine, you should disconnect the battery from the engine. Inadvertently hooking an ohmmeter to a live circuit will at least blow its internal fuse or (on some of the smaller, less expensive units that may be unfused) burn out the meter.

Take special note that some engines equipped with tachometers use an electrical signal from the charging system to measure engine revolutions per minute. You

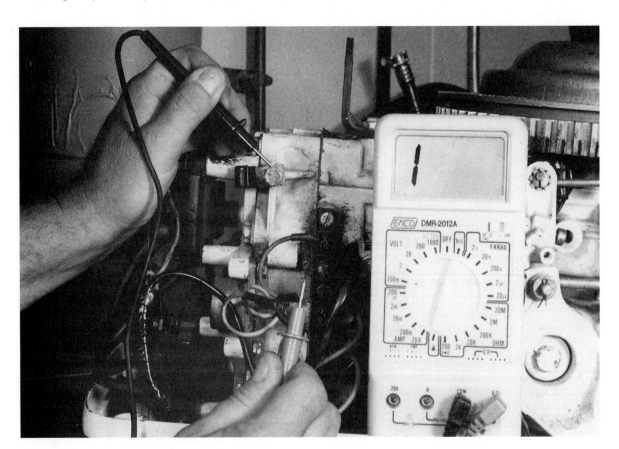

Figure 6-2. *An ohmmeter tests a rectifier diode for current flow in one direction.*

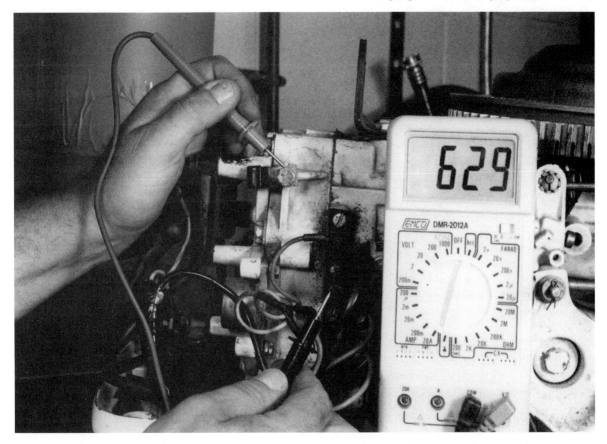

Figure 6-3. *The rectifier shown in Figure 6-2 being tested for current flow in the opposite direction.*

should check your service manual for any special instructions regarding disconnecting this lead from the charging system (often hooked to the regulator or rectifier) before performing tests to these components to eliminate this circuit as a possible cause for charging-system problems.

To test your rectifier, you'll need to separate the wiring connections between it and the stator windings. Simply follow the wires to the point where they connect to leads coming from under the flywheel. Label the wires to ensure correct reassembly, and disconnect the leads at this point.

Then, with your ohmmeter set to the low-ohms scale, simply check each diode lead for continuity in one direction. Reverse the meter leads on the same two connections and check for continuity in the other direction of flow. There should be a reading of nearly

0 ohms in one direction (a very low resistance reading is normal, as diodes do offer some electrical resistance) and a reading of infinity when your meter leads are reversed. Any variation from these readings means the rectifier is defective and must be replaced.

Testing the Stator Windings

To test the stator windings you will need to use your ohmmeter again. Be sure the wire leads to the rectifier are separated, as they were for the rectifier test. To check your stator, you need to confirm continuity through its windings, and to be sure there's no short circuit to ground in any of the windings.

Your meter should be set to the low-ohms scale for the continuity tests, and the high-ohms scale for the

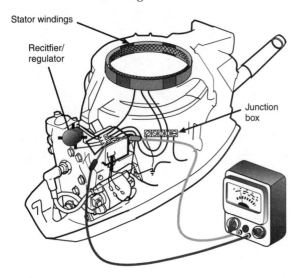

Stator windings

Recitfier/
regulator

Junction
box

Figure 6-4. *Testing the stator windings for continuity.*

short-to-ground test. In all cases, you will be dealing with three wires for stator testing. One of these wires will have a common connection to the other two, and so testing from this common lead to each of the other two will give a resistance value as specified in your workshop manual.

If the reading you get for either of these checks is greater than specification, or shows infinity, indicating a break in the winding somewhere, the flywheel will have to be removed and the stator replaced. This should be done by your dealer, as special tools will be required to remove the flywheel, and in some cases to properly position the new stator winding.

To check your stator for a short circuit to ground, switch your meter to the high-ohms scale. Next, hook one of the meter's test leads to a good engine ground, and the other to the previously identified "common" lead from the stator. Your meter should read infinity. If not, your stator windings have a breakdown in their insulation somewhere, and will have to be replaced.

I should tell you that stator winding failure is extremely rare. There are, however, two main contributing causes to early failure. The first is extreme engine overheating, when the winding insulation actually melts. The second is improper service to an engine that has been accidentally submerged in salt water. See Chapter 10 for details on how to deal with this unfortunate situation.

The Sequence to Follow.   To round off this section on charging systems, here's a useful sequence to follow when you're analyzing problems: (*Note: Make sure your problem isn't something as simple as a blown fuse in the circuit. Your service manual's wiring diagram for the starter circuit will help you locate this fuse.*)

1. As with all electrical problems, check for corrosion and loose connections.
2. Verify the condition of your battery, and its suitability for your boat. Compare amp-hour capacity with the electrical draw of the equipment you have on board. The battery may be too small to handle the accessories you've added over the years.
3. Apply the three-step voltage test to your system.
4. If no charge is indicated, begin by performing the ohmmeter tests described for your rectifier/regulator. This is usually the problem.
5. If the rectifier checks out okay, perform the ohmmeter tests described for the stator windings.

By performing the checks in this sequence, you'll always be able to pinpoint charging system problems with your outboard engine.

Troubleshooting Electric Starter Circuits

First let's have a quick look at Figure 6-5 to see what we're talking about. The illustration shows a typical starter circuit on a outboard engine with remote controls. But be aware that not all engines have the remote control harness plug in the location shown here. On many installations, the harness plug is located under the engine cowl.

If your outboard engine doesn't have remote controls, it will simply have a starter button on the engine. It may also have a neutral safety switch integrated with the mechanical gear-shift linkage under the cowl cover. A simplified wiring diagram of this circuit is shown in Figure 6-6.

It should be pointed out that your engine may have some of these connections at a wiring junction box. Also, starter circuits are commonly used by manufacturers to add extra wires feeding additional circuits on

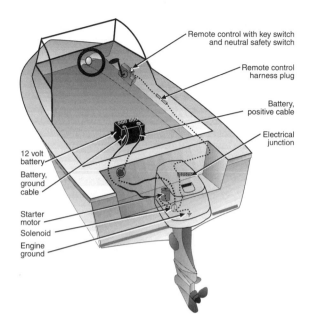

Remote control with key switch
and neutral safety switch

Remote control
harness plug

Battery,
positive cable

Electrical
junction

12 volt
battery

Battery,
ground
cable

Starter
motor

Solenoid

Engine
ground

Figure 6-5. *An overview of a remotely controlled starter circuit.*

your engine—so refer to your engine's specific diagram, and narrow it down to what you see in this drawing. These are the only components you should be focusing on if your troubles are starter-related.

All outboard engines use what is referred to as an inertia type of starter motor. Midsize and large engines

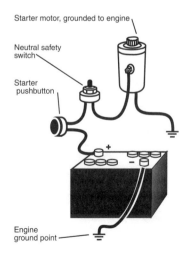

Starter motor, grounded to engine

Neutral safety
switch

Starter
pushbutton

+

−

Engine
ground point

Figure 6-6. *The integrated starter circuit.*

also employ a remotely mounted solenoid. Unlike automotive starters, these units rely on the inertia created by the spinning starter motor to "throw" the starter drive gear upward, engaging it with the teeth of the flywheel ring gear. Often, the problem with these systems is simply that the starter spins too slowly to engage the drive gear. Slow spinning can be caused by a weak battery, or an electrical connection that is loose or corroded, causing excessive resistance in the circuit.

So, as with the charging system, the first thing for you to check is the power source—the battery, and all its related connections. Perform the "open circuit voltage test" described earlier under Battery Testing to determine its state of charge. If needed, charge the battery to bring it up to snuff before proceeding with any circuit tests. Of all the electrical circuits found on your boat, the starter probably draws the greatest amperage when cranking, so it needs all the battery can give until the engine starts.

Once you are certain your battery is fully charged, you can begin tracing circuits. To test the smaller integrated system found on low-powered engines without remote controls, you will check for voltage at points throughout the circuit at the correct time.

Figure 6-7 shows the points to check in numerical sequence, but before you begin, make sure your engine ground point and the ground bolt or strap (the heavy black cable) are corrosion-free, and the mounting bolts tight.

Begin at Point 1, checking the power source to the push-button switch. While your meter's black test lead makes contact with a good ground on your engine (the bolt or cable grounding the starter motor to the engine is a good point, or you could ground directly to the battery negative terminal if the battery is located close to the engine) you will probe through the circuit with the red test lead from the meter.

Point 1. The voltage reading here should be very nearly the same as the direct reading across the battery. If not, there is a bad or broken connection between the battery and the connection at Point 1. If the voltage reading is good here, proceed to:

Point 2. At this point you should also disable the ignition system to prevent the engine from starting as you perform the next four tests. Now press in the starter button while holding your red test lead probe on Point 2. You should get a reading of approximately 12 volts. If not, your starter button is defective and will

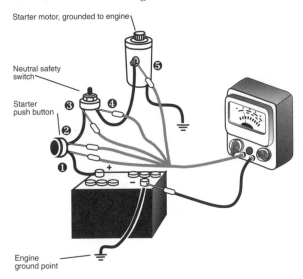

Figure 6-7. *Voltage check points for the integrated circuit.*

need replacement. If 12 volts is present at Point 2, proceed to:

Point 3. Again, with the starter button depressed, you should get a 12-volt reading. If not, the connection is bad, or the wire connecting the push-button switch to the neutral safety switch has a break in it. Repair or replace as needed. Next, be certain the engine is in the neutral position and move your meter probe to:

Point 4. With the starter button engaged, you should get a 12-volt reading at this point. If not, then the neutral switch is either defective or out of adjustment. To check for an adjustment problem, use a small screwdriver and manually depress the safety switch button completely. If that doesn't give you a 12-volt reading at Point 4, the switch must be replaced.

If depressing the switch with a screwdriver does give you 12 volts at Point 4, you need to adjust the neutral safety switch. Reposition it in its mount so that the shift control linkage will normally depress the button all the way, providing 12 volts at Point 4.

If you do get a 12-volt reading at Point 4 it means the circuit is fine all the way so far. But if the starter motor is still not cranking, move your voltmeter's red test probe to:

Point 5. Check for 12 volts at this point with the engine in neutral and the starter button depressed. If 12 volts isn't present at this point, there is poor connection

or a broken wire between Points 4 and 5. Repair or replace as required.

If you do get 12 volts at Point 5, then the problem is in the starter motor, and you'll have to remove it for rebuilding or replacement.

Voltage-Drop Test. Another simple test that can help you locate any points in a starter circuit that could cause resistance to electrical flow, and result in slow cranking (or no cranking at all) is called the "voltage-drop" test. You'll use your multimeter set to the low-volts scale (if it's not self-scaling) to perform the entire test. This test is best done with a digital voltmeter as you will be checking for readings of 0.3 volt or less. It will enable you to isolate bad connections, undersized wiring, or faulty components within the circuit.

Figure 6-8 shows the meter hook-ups for this test. Before you begin, locate the connections labeled "A" and "B." "A" is the feed from the ignition switch (or start button) that powers the solenoid when the key or button is engaged. "B" is the ground for the magnetic coil in the solenoid. It has a black wire.

Begin by verifying that connection "B" is well grounded. With the key off, use your ohmmeter to check for continuity (a reading of 0 on your meter) between the connection and ground on the engine block. If your reading varies, repair connection "B," or replace the wire.

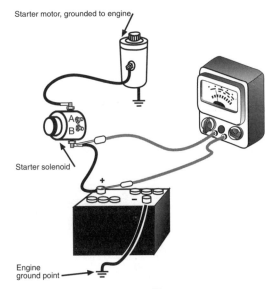

Figure 6-8. *Starter circuit voltage-drop test—Step 1.*

Next, with the key in the crank position, check for 12 volts at connection "A." If 12 volts is not present, the problem is somewhere in the feed line from your starter switch or neutral safety switch. Follow the steps described below to correct this problem. If all seems well here, you may proceed with the voltage drop test.

For each of the four steps in this test, the engine must be cranking.

Step 1. Hook up the multimeter as shown in Figure 6-8. Your voltage reading with the engine cranking should not exceed 0.3 volt. If it does, then:

1. The connection at the positive battery post is bad; or
2. The connection right at the solenoid is bad; or
3. The battery cable is too thin and must be upgraded to a larger cable. An easy way to check this is to feel the battery cable as you crank the engine over. If it gets warm to the touch, it's too small.

For engines of 15 hp and under, with a distance of less than 10 feet (3 m) from the starter motor to the battery, wire size #10 on the American Wire Gauge scale (10 AWG) is usually adequate.

For these same engines, runs of 10 to 15 feet (3 to 5 m) need wire of 8 AWG.

Runs of 16 to 20 feet (5 to 7 m) need 6 AWG.

On engines in the 20 to 30 hp range, use 6 AWG, 4 AWG and 3 AWG respectively for the same cable runs.

On the larger engines (V4s and V6s) use 4 AWG, 2 AWG, and 1 AWG respectively.

Use this quick-reference table to check your battery cable:

Starter Motor to Battery Cable Sizes

Engine HP	Wiring Run	AWG #
15 or less	10 ft. (3 m) or less	10
15 or less	10 to 15 ft. (3 to 5 m)	8
15 or less	16 to 20 ft. (5 to 7 m)	6
20 to 30	10 ft. (3 m) or less	6
20 to 30	10 to 15 ft. (3 to 5 m)	4
20 to 30	16 to 20 ft. (5 to 7 m)	3
Over 30	10 ft. (3 m) or less	4
Over 30	10 to 15 ft. (3 to 5 m)	2
Over 30	16 to 20 ft. (5 to 7 m)	1

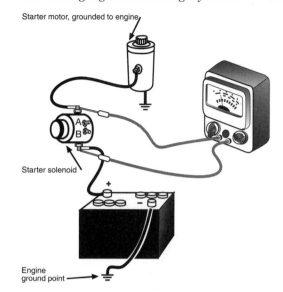

Figure 6-9. *Starter circuit voltage-drop test—Step 2.*

Step 2. Now it's time to check the voltage drop through the solenoid. It's important that you don't connect the voltmeter leads as shown in Figure 6-9 until the engine is cranking. If you connect up when the engine isn't being cranked, you risk damage to your voltmeter.

A reading here in excess of 0.2 volt indicates a fault inside the solenoid, and it will have to be replaced. Again, make sure to disconnect the voltmeter before you stop cranking the engine at this point.

Step 3. If all's well so far, the next step is to check for a voltage drop between the solenoid and the starter motor. Connect the voltmeter as shown in Figure 6-10. Crank the engine and watch your voltmeter. The reading should not exceed 0.2 volt.

If it does, the connection at the solenoid or the starter motor may be bad; or (as with the battery cables) the wire connecting the solenoid to the starter may be too thin—it should be the same size as the main battery-feed wire.

Step 4. Finally, we'll check for a voltage drop at the end of the run, at the starter motor itself. Hook up the meter as shown in Figure 6-11 and turn the key to the crank position. Your voltage-drop reading should be less than 0.3 volt. Again, if the reading is above this, either a connection is bad at the engine or negative

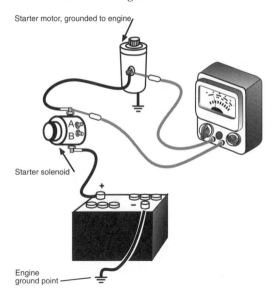

Figure 6-10. *Starter circuit voltage-drop test—Step 3.*

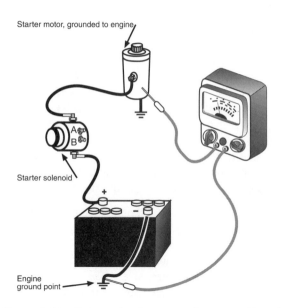

Figure 6-11. *Starter circuit voltage-drop test—Step 4.*

battery post or the cable is undersized—it should be the same size as the main positive-feed cable.

Testing the Neutral Safety Switch

If your engine is equipped with remote controls, the neutral safety switch is probably located inside the control unit. It prevents your starting the engine if the gearshift is in forward or reverse. The starter motor will work only if the gearshift is in neutral.

The remote-control unit is a complicated piece of machinery, so don't even attempt to diagnose problems that lead to the neutral switch without a factory workshop manual for your engine and control unit. There are just too many variables in wire colors and control-unit disassembly procedures to cover here.

In fact, unless you're a fairly competent mechanic, I'd advise you to leave the remote-control unit well alone. It's full of spring-loaded levers, shims, and cable attachments that are absolutely critical in their placement and precise function, so beware.

The good news is that it's quite easy to check all wiring and components affected by this switch, so you can talk intelligently to your dealer's mechanic about the problem.

In the electrical circuit, your neutral safety switch lies between the ignition switch and the starter motor solenoid. When you shift the control unit into neutral, the safety switch should be in the "closed" position, completing the circuit between the ignition switch and the terminal marked "A" in Figure 6-8.

So, the quick way to check the switch is to look for a 12-volt reading on your voltmeter at this terminal with the key in the "crank" position. Just touch your meter's black lead to a good ground, and the red lead to this terminal. Then have someone turn the key to the crank position with the shift in neutral.

If you get no reading when the key is turned to crank, the problem is probably within the remote-control unit—but not necessarily. There could be corrosion at the remote-control harness plug shown in Figure 6-5, or there could be a break in the wire coming from the plug assembly to the stern of the boat. Using your wiring diagram as a guide, identify this solenoid feed wire positively.

Next, disconnect the wire from the solenoid and identify which terminal it goes to in the plug assembly. Use your ohmmeter set to the low-ohms scale to check for continuity between these two points. (Incidentally, you may need to create an extended jumper lead from your alligator clips to extend one of the test leads from

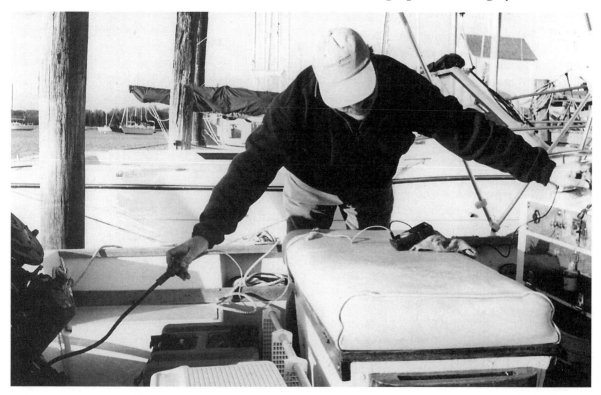

Figure 6-12. *Extension harness ohmmeter test.*

your meter, depending on the distance involved.) You should get a reading of nearly zero on your meter if this wire is intact from the plug to the engine.

If you get a high reading, or a reading of infinity, then there is a break in the wire between the plug and the engine. Depending upon your particular installation, this may mean replacing the factory-supplied extension harness as a unit. If your boat's wire feed from the control unit to the engine is a series of individual wires wrapped in electrical tape or plastic tie-wraps, you should be able to trace the harness and find the chafe point with the break. Repair or replace as required. If you get a low-resistance reading near zero, then the problem is in the remote-control unit itself, and should be attended to by your dealer. Figure 6-12 shows the extension harness being tested with an ohmmeter in a typical installation.

Neutral Switch Misadjustment. Testing for neutral switch misadjustment is quite simple. Hold the

shift control lever with one hand and the ignition key with the other. Hold the key in the crank position and gently work the shift lever to its extremes in the neutral position.

If you hear the starter try to engage, either the switch is badly adjusted, or the remote-control mechanism is badly worn and needs to be serviced by your dealer. Don't be surprised if the control mechanism needs replacement. Excessive wear of internal parts is common on older units.

Testing an Ignition Switch

Like neutral switches, most ignition switches are placed inside the remote-control unit. This makes testing difficult, but some of the procedures used to test the neutral switch apply equally to the ignition switch.

What you need to find out about this switch is whether a 12-volt current is getting to it, and leaving it, at the correct times. You can test for this outside the unit, up to the point where the main plug assembly enters the control box.

If the main wiring harness connecting the engine to the remote-control box is in good condition, which you can check visually by tracing it from the engine, up under the side coaming of the boat to the control box, then problems are most likely within the control box itself.

All manufacturers provide good descriptions of the function of each terminal in the main harness-plug assembly, and all provide a test sequence using an ohmmeter to verify continuity between terminals on this plug with the key in certain positions.

A good quick check using your voltmeter can also be made however.

Begin by verifying that 12 volts is being sent to the ignition switch from the engine. Use your engine's wiring diagram to identify the power-feed terminal from the engine to the main plug on the engine side of the circuit. (Hint: This wire is usually fed by a jumper lead that comes from the starter solenoid, or a wiring junction box bolted to the side of the engine block. Also, the terminal within the plug assembly will generally be much larger in diameter than all the others.)

If 12 volts is getting to this plug, and the plug terminals are in good visual condition, it is reasonable to assume that with the plug connected, 12 volts is getting into the control box assembly and presumably feeding one side of the ignition switch.

On older engines, a wire coming from the remote-control unit will provide 12 volts to the ignition module (CDI unit). This 12-volt current powers the electronic circuitry in the module while the engine's running. Use your engine wiring diagram to identify this wire on your engine. See Figure 6-13.

New engine ignition modules are powered by the charge coil under the engine's flywheel and have no power feed from the ignition switch. Check your engine's wiring diagram.

Once you've identified it, make sure the emergency shut-off switch is de-activated and turn the ignition key to the "on" position. If you get a reading of 12 volts at the point where this wire attaches to the ignition module, you know that this function of the ignition switch is okay.

If you don't get a 12-volt reading, you need to trace the main harness, looking for trouble spots. Possible

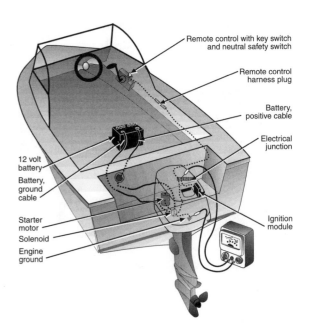

Figure 6-13. *Checking for voltage from the ignition switch to the ignition module. Ignition key must be on.*

trouble spots could be ones like the point where you drilled a hole through the harness while you were mounting that new rodholder or downrigger mount. If you can't see any trouble spots, then the problem is in the control unit.

In addition to the 12-volt current going to your engine's ignition module, as mentioned earlier, you need to have 12 volts at one of the starter solenoid's small terminals. At least, you need it there when the key is in the "crank" position and the gearshift is in neutral. All manufacturers use a colored wire for this connection—OMC and Mercury frequently use a yellow-and-red wire here. Remember that the black wire from the solenoid is a ground lead, so it's not the one you need to check. Use the test procedure described earlier to check for voltage at this point.

If you get 12 volts at this connection while the key is in the crank position, you know that the ignition switch is okay. If you don't get 12 volts, trace the harness as you did for the other wires, and if no visual damage can be found the problem is inside the control box. Figure 6-14 shows the solenoid terminal being checked for 12 volts with the key in the "crank" position.

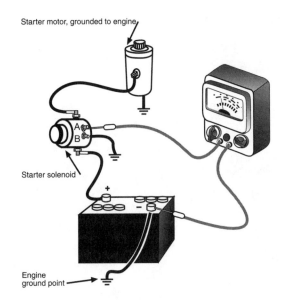

Starter motor, grounded to engine

Starter solenoid

A
B

Engine
ground point

Figure 6-14. *Starter solenoid voltage check.*

I should point out that the remote-control box also houses switches for electrically activated choking mechanisms, tilt-and-trim mechanisms, and other systems. Tests for these circuits will be discussed in later chapters of this book.

Other Starter-Related Problems. In addition to problems normally associated with electrical faults in the starter circuit, such as slow cranking or no cranking at all, some severe mechanical troubles may prevent the starter motor from turning the engine over. One symptom is a loud "clunk" as the starter drive gear engages the flywheel with full force—only to encounter an engine that will not spin. Or, in the case of a manual starter, the pull cord may not budge more than a few inches no matter how hard you pull.

There are three possible causes for this symptom, and they're all bad.

First, because of a cooling system problem, the engine may have overheated so much that the pistons have expanded and stuck fast in their respective cylinders.

Second, a lack of lubrication might have led to an overheating condition or piston seizure. This could be caused by an improper fuel-to-oil mix, through either human error or failure of the automatic oiling system.

Third, the engine's cylinders might have water in

them, causing a hydraulic lock. This could be caused by a head gasket that is leaking internally, or a cracked cylinder head or block.

In any event, if the clunk symptom occurs, or you can't pull out the starter cord on your engine, you'll need to check to see if the engine is actually seized.

To do this, disable the ignition system and remove the engine cover so you can get to the flywheel. Try to turn it by hand—but be careful, it may be extremely hot if the seizure was caused by overheating. If the flywheel won't move, the worst has happened.

Your next step is to remove the spark plugs and try to spin the engine over. If it does spin, and water comes spraying out of any of the spark plug holes, then it's likely to be the fault of the head gasket, or a cracked cylinder head—possibilities we discussed above.

But if the engine still won't spin, let it cool down completely and try again. If it spins now, you'll know the seizure was only temporary, caused by extreme overheating. The fact that it will turn over now still doesn't exclude internal damage, however. You should get your dealer to remove the cylinder heads and inspect the cylinders for damage. If there is none, you can feel quite lucky. But you must make sure you correct the cause of the overheating before you run the engine again. (See Chapter 9.)

If the engine will still not crank over after you've let it cool down, and you still can't get it to budge by working the flywheel, serious internal damage has occurred. You need expert help, and possibly a complete engine teardown.

Manual Starters

If you have a small outboard engine, it's probably equipped with the familiar pull-cord starter mechanism. If yours hasn't failed yet, it will. Sooner or later, all that pulling and yanking will take its toll on this assembly and cause it to malfunction. If you're lucky, the problem will be as simple as a broken cord. If you're unlucky, it will be a snapped recoil spring.

In either case, you might be able to save the day by using either the emergency pull cord found in many engines, or by making one from a piece of rope. If you can get to the flywheel, wrap the cord around in a clockwise direction and give it a strong pull. This will usually get the engine running.

The problem with trying to create a generic cure for these problems lies in the multiplicity of pull-cord systems. In addition, depending upon the manufacturer, you may need special tools to replace the recoil spring safely. This is an area you should not jump into without the aid of the factory manual.

Besides the frustration that often goes along with replacement of the recoil spring, you need to be careful of its sudden unwinding, a serious safety consideration. Always wear eye protection when working with a recoil starter assembly. Also, it's a good idea to disable the ignition system to avoid the possibility of the engine starting as you turn the flywheel while working on these assemblies.

Having said all that, I'll now relent. Here's how to deal with pull cord replacement and recoil spring service on one of the popular recoil assemblies used by Johnson and Evinrude on their 9.9 and 15 hp engines.

Winding On a New Pull Cord. On most engines, replacing the pull cord is a matter of simply pulling what's left of the cord off the drum. You pull it out and off, against the recoil-spring tension, until the knot in the end of the cord is exposed.

At this point, you must somehow lock the drum assembly in place while you cut the knot off and remove the cord from the drum. Keep in mind that in this position, the recoil spring is at its maximum tension. It will desperately want to spring back into its relaxed position. Usually, a screwdriver or a tapered piece of wood can be wedged into position between the drum and a fixed part of the engine for long enough to accomplish this task.

Figure 6-15 shows the drum assembly being held in place on a Johnson 9.9 hp engine. Once the old cord has been removed from the pulley drum you'll need to purchase a length of the correct cord from your dealer. Use only approved replacement cord for these assemblies, as it has been tested for strength, and it's the right diameter to fit your pulley/drum assembly. The exact length of the cord will always be specified in your engine workshop manual.

Next, pry the concealing cap off the pull-cord handle with a small screwdriver if you intend to reuse it. This will expose the knot at the end of the cord. Use the small screwdriver to pry the knot up and out of the handle. Then simply pull whatever is left of the cord through the handle.

Figure 6-15. *Removing a broken pull cord.*

Now, fuse approximately ½ inch (13 mm) of each end of the new cord by passing the cord carefully over an open flame, and tie a tight figure-of-eight knot in one end of the new cord.

Figure 6-16 illustrates this knot on a new pull cord. Feed all the new cord through the handle and push the

Figure 6-16. *The figure-of-eight knot to use on all starter cords.*

fully feed the new cord through the hole in the drum/pulley. Be very careful as you do this work not to disturb the wedge you have positioned to lock the recoil in the unwound position.

After sliding the cord through the hole, tie a tight figure-of-eight knot in this end and position it in any recess the manufacturer has provided for it. Finally, while keeping a firm hold on the cord, remove your locking wedge. Let the drum ease itself back slowly, and feed the cord onto it. If all is well, the recoil spring will pull the cord right into place. If you paid careful attention to the cord length specified in your workshop manual, the handle on the pull cord will retract completely and fit snugly in place. If it doesn't, you may have to shorten the cord slightly. Figure 6-17 shows the new pull cord being wound on.

On any recoil system that gives you access to the knot at the center of the pulley or drum assembly without your having to partially disassemble the recoil mechanism, the procedure I've described here will work just fine for replacement of the pull cord.

knot tightly down into place with your screwdriver. Reinstall the knot cover in the handle, then thread the new cord through the positioning hole in your engine cover and lead it to the recoil starter assembly. Care-

Figure 6-17. *Winding on a new pull cord.*

Replacing the Recoil Spring. To replace the recoil spring, the starter assembly will have to be removed from the engine. Begin by prying the knot cover from the pull-cord handle and untying the knot in the end. Carefully allow the recoil spring to pull the cord through the hole in the engine cover. If the spring is broken, simply pull the cord through the positioning hole.

Now unthread the single nut that holds the starter assembly to the engine-mounting bracket. This nut is located in the center of the very top of the starter assembly. Don't lift the bolt out of the assembly, but use it to help hold together the pull-cord pulley and the metal recoil-spring housing. You'll be carefully lifting the assembly out and away from the engine.

Be extremely careful not to let the lower spring housing separate from the plastic drum and pulley assembly. Separation of these two components at this point will guarantee that the spring will come flying out of the engine at you. Once you've removed it, it's a good idea to mount the whole unit in a vise on its side

with the vise jaws clamping on the head of the mounting bolt and the other end of the bolt protruding from the bottom of the assembly. Use a soft jaw or soft wooden block against the threaded end of the bolt to prevent damaging the threads.

Once the starter assembly is securely mounted in a vise, grasp the end of the recoil spring that will be visible protruding from a small slot in the side of the metal spring housing. Carefully pull the spring out of the housing with the pliers until it is completely unwound.

Next, remove the assembly from the vise and separate the plastic pulley and pinion-gear assembly from the metal spring housing. Remove the remainder of the spring from the inside of the housing. Clean all parts and inspect for wear, replacing as needed. But note that the pinion-gear teeth are supposed to be rounded at the upper end of each tooth. This helps them to engage with the flywheel. Rounding is neither a sign of wear nor cause for replacement.

The next step is to install the new recoil spring into its housing with the spacer washer and spring retainer

Figure 6-18. *Installing the new recoil spring.*

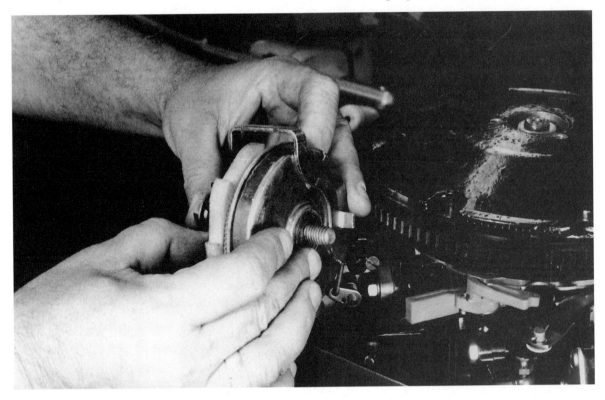

Figure 6-19. *Reinstalling the assembled unit on the engine.*

in place as shown in Figure 6-18. Be sure to lubricate the inside of the spring housing with some white lithium grease. Once the spring's in place, install the rewind pulley, making sure the small pin on the bottom of the pulley engages with the bent-over loop in the end of the recoil spring.

Now reposition the pinion gear on the pulley. Don't put any grease on the spiral gear the pinion fits over because it could cause the unit to bind. These parts are designed to be self-lubricating. You should, however, lightly lube the center mounting bolt with some engine oil and install it through the center of the unit, making sure all washers and shims are in their proper positions. For this particular unit, a 3/8-inch coarse-thread nut can now be threaded on the lower end of the bolt to hold the assembly together while you wind in the new spring.

Next, reinstall the pull cord and wrap it tightly around the pulley in a counterclockwise direction as you look down at the pulley. Hold the metal spring housing firmly, and slowly pull the cord out from the

unit, turning the pulley in a counterclockwise direction. Carefully feed the recoil spring into the slot in the side of the housing as the pulley turns, helping it along with a slight push if needed. Continue until the recoil spring end loop reaches the side of the metal housing. Once this is done, rewind the pull cord around the pulley in a counterclockwise direction.

Reinstall the spring for the pinion gear as it was before disassembly, then remove the $\frac{3}{8}$-inch nut from the mounting bolt, being careful to hold all the pieces firmly together. Thoroughly clean the threads on the mounting bolt if you haven't already, and install some thread-locking compound to the threads.

Carefully position the assembly on the mounting bracket. Be sure to place the positioning tab of the spring housing in the hole on the mounting bracket so this unit can't slip once the center bolt is tightened. Figure 6-19 shows the assembly being repositioned on the mounting bracket of the engine. Once everything is in place, tighten the mounting bolt.

Now you have to push the pull cord through the

hole in the engine cover and reattach the handle. As a last check on this particular engine, you need to be certain the starter lockout lever (the red plastic piece) is functioning as it should. A common mistake is to position incorrectly the spring that activates this lever. Check for normal operation of this feature and reposition the spring if necessary. Recoil spring replacement is now complete.

In closing, it must be emphasized that the procedure described here is for this particular recoil type. If you don't have one of these engines, your system will be entirely different, and specific procedures will have to be followed in accordance with your engine's workshop manual. If your manual calls for special tools to accomplish this task, take the engine to your dealer. Experience shows that if you attempt to get away without using the tools required, you'll be in for a very unpleasant day.

Chapter 7

The Fuel and Lubrication Systems

Without question, the fuel and lubrication systems are two of the most important supplying your engine with its basic needs. Also without question is the fact that most cases of poor running, or no running at all, are caused by problems with fuel.

In spite of your best efforts at maintenance, water, dirt, and gum can enter your fuel system and cause problems. But if you follow the advice in this chapter, you'll know how to deal with fuel problems, and you can also be confident that your engine's lubrication system is operating as it should.

Fuel-Delivery Systems

Figure 7-1 shows two common fuel systems. The first has a removable tank. The second, a system found on larger boats, has a built-in tank system similar to the one shown in dotted lines in Figure 7-1.

A third system consists of the integral fuel tank found on the smallest dinghy engines. It's a simple, gravity-feed system, with a tank mounted to the engine block, a simple shut-off valve for the fuel leaving the tank, a fuel strainer, and a carburetor assembly. It requires no fuel pump or primer bulb, although on some of the newest small engines, a diaphragm-type fuel pump has been incorporated in the carburetor. This

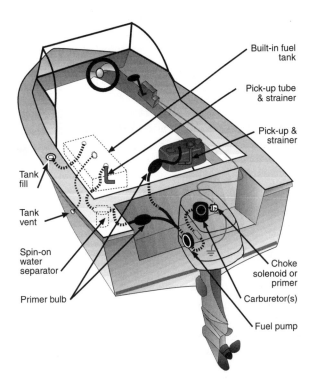

Figure 7-1. *An overview of the fuel system, showing portable and built-in tanks.*

- Built-in fuel tank
- Pick-up tube & strainer
- Pick-up & strainer
- Tank fill
- Tank vent
- Spin-on water separator
- Primer bulb
- Choke solenoid or primer
- Carburetor(s)
- Fuel pump

type is easily recognized because the carburetor has an additional hose (besides the fuel delivery hose) going to it. The additional hose comes from a fitting on the side of the engine crankcase.

The fuel system begins at the fuel tank. Whether it's built-in or removable, the tank has the same potential for problems. One of the most common problems is water accumulating in the tank. It's caused by moisture condensing from the air in a partially filled tank.

Sometimes, though, the water is in the fuel when you buy it. Conscientious dealers constantly check their tanks for water and contamination, but some just don't take the time to bother. This means it's quite possible for you to buy gas containing a high concentration of water, right at the fuel dock. This happens mostly during spring and fall, when significant changes in temperature from day to night cause the maximum amount of condensation in the dealer's tanks.

Eventually this water will begin to create rust on the inside of the painted-steel portable fuel tanks traditionally supplied by outboard engine manufacturers. In time, the rust will begin to flake off, and what's not caught by the built-in strainer will be sucked into the engine. Most of it will be stopped by the fuel filter/water separator found on most large engine installations, but even these filters can't stop some of the microscopic rust particles. They'll eventually end up inside your engine's carburetor(s), plugging the jets and tiny passages. This is when the first symptoms of trouble may appear—rough engine idle, loss of power, and perhaps even reluctance to run at all.

Aluminum tanks are often used for permanent tanks below deck, and they certainly won't rust in the way steel does. But aluminum does eventually begin to oxidize or corrode, generating its own microscopic particles to mix with the fuel.

Plastic tanks are available as both portable and built-in installations, and they eliminate particulate matter from tank deterioration as a source of problems. But they still don't eliminate rust, dirt, or water from your supplier's tank. And, unfortunately, plastic tanks are almost as susceptible to the problems of condensation as metal tanks.

Since there's no way you can guarantee uncontaminated fuel from your tank, the bottom line with all fuel systems is that you must use adequate and properly sized fuel filters and water separators. All manufacturers list these items in their accessory catalogs, and I'd highly recommend that you add one of the spin-on fuel/water separators shown in Figure 7-1, even on a small engine. These elements provide a simple way to check for excess water build-up in the system, as well as an easy way to take a fuel sample from your tank.

The Spin-On Fuel/Water Separator

Checking or replacing the spin-on water separator is easy. Simply spin the element off, holding a bucket beneath it to catch spilled fuel. Use a clockwise force to loosen the element, as you look at it from above. Drain the element into the bucket and look for water, which will separate from the fuel into globules, and for any dark-brown rust particles.

When you replace the element, check to make sure the old sealing ring came off the mount. Just as with oil filters, spinning on a new element over an old seal is sure to cause a severe leak.

These elements should be changed at least once a season, or perhaps twice if you use your boat frequently. Inspect the fuel sample for signs of trouble at each change. You can expect years of service free of trouble from water or rust build-up if you conscientiously maintain this filter.

Fuel System Safety Considerations

Because of the extremely flammable nature of outboard engine fuel, tank installations must incorporate special safety features. This is especially true of built-in tanks, where many potential problems will be hidden. You should note that boat fuel tanks and installations are regulated by U.S. Coast Guard (USCG) safety standards, and any deviation from these standards is not only illegal but could be extremely dangerous to you and your passengers. If your boat has a yellow, black, and white Boating Industry Association (BIA—since 1979, the NMMA) and USCG certification plate attached near the transom, rest assured that the fuel system has been installed to a safe standard.

Let's begin with the built-in fuel tank, as represented by the dotted lines in Figure 7-1. You'll notice that in addition to the tank itself, you can see the filler-cap fitting on deck, and the hose connecting it to the tank. Also, there is a smaller hose connecting the tank to a fitting that must vent excess fuel or fumes outside the hull.

There is also, of course, the hose that supplies fuel to the engine. All marine fuel hoses must meet specific standards, not only for compatibility with the fuel used, but also for fire resistance. This precludes the use of most automotive-grade flexible fuel hose. In general, without getting into a lengthy explanation of the code, let me urge you to be certain that any flexible (rubber) fuel hose installed on your boat has the words "Approved, USCG type" embossed on it.

All fuel-hose clamps must be made completely of stainless steel. Don't be fooled by the standard clamp purchased at your auto parts store. It may have a stainless band, but the screw mechanism on it is more than likely plated steel. It will rust on a boat and eventually fail. Check all fuel-system clamps, hoses, and connecting fittings at least annually to be sure they're tight and showing no sign of leakage.

The regulations also call for all metallic parts of the fuel tank and deck fill to be electrically grounded, to minimize the possibility of sparking when the fill nozzle touches the deck fitting. This is generally done with a green wire attached to the back of the deck-fill fixture and connected to a tab on the fuel tank near the fill-pipe connection. These wires frequently corrode and break off, rendering the grounding system useless and unsafe. Check these connections periodically to be sure of their integrity.

Fuel-System Basics and Common Problems

One of the most frequent fuel-system problems is a blockage in the tank's vent fitting or hose. You'll know if there's a problem here if you have constant trouble filling your tank without fuel surging out of the fill pipe. Usually, the blockage occurs when the fine-meshed screen built into the vent fitting begins to corrode—or when saltwater installations get clogged with salt, preventing the vent from "breathing" properly.

Vent screens can be cleaned by scraping away the build-up with a pocket knife, but sometimes they get too encrusted with salt, and need replacement. Always be sure this vent is clear to do its job because it affects the way your engine runs as well as the way your fuel tank gets filled.

On most portable tanks, the vent is located in the fill cap and is either unscrewed to open, or, on some tanks, simply pulled up to snap open. A third type of tank vent has a hidden vent that allows air to enter only when a slight vacuum is created in the tank.

This design is intended to eliminate the possibility of gas vapors escaping through the vent into the atmosphere. The vent lies under the point where you plug the fuel hose to the tank. It's a small opening connected to a diaphragm-type, one-way valve inside the tank on the bottom side of the gauge assembly. As a vacuum is formed in the tank, this valve opens and air is drawn into the tank to allow fuel to escape. Once an adequate amount of air enters the tank, the valve closes. A problem with this type of vent is that the small opening on the gauge housing must be kept clear—but it's located where oil, dirt, and dust are certain to accumulate, causing a restriction in the vent system. If you have a "non-vented" tank, be sure to check this opening periodically to make sure it's not plugged with dirt and debris. If the vent isn't working, or if there's a kink in the hose connecting it to the fuel tank, a vacuum will form inside the tank and prevent fuel from getting to the engine. The symptoms would be the same as those caused by running out of fuel, even with a full tank.

Fuel-Tank Strainer. Another item to consider with a permanent fuel tank is the fuel pickup strainer inside the tank. You can usually reach the area where the strainer sits by removing a deck plate, or perhaps a cover inside a center-console. Once removed, the fuel fill pipe, fuel gauge sender, tank vent connection, and fuel delivery system will be exposed.

In some cases, the fuel delivery pipe is an integral part of the sending unit, and by removing the fastening screws that hold the sender to the tank and lifting the unit up and out, you can reach the strainer on the end of a long fuel pickup tube that protrudes down to near the tank's bottom. This strainer screen will be made of either a fine nylon mesh or a metal mesh of either stainless or brass. This screen should be inspected at least annually and, if dirty, should be cleaned.

In many cases, the fuel delivery tube is screwed or even welded into place on the tank, and access to the pickup screen isn't possible as part of routine service.

Anti-Siphon Valve. On many installations, your fuel pickup tube may also have an anti-siphon valve installed in-line with the fuel delivery tube. Anti-siphon systems are mandatory as part of permanent tank safety requirements. But these valves have been so problematic in some instances that some manufacturers even recommended removing them. This should be done by the dealer.

Another method builders use to prevent siphoning is to mount and secure all fuel lines above the highest fuel level in the tank, with the boat floating in its normal position. This anti-siphon feature is important. It will prevent the fuel tank from draining into the bilge of your boat in the event a leak develops in the feed line to your engine. Never make any modifications to the original positions of the fuel lines in your boat; and if your tank pickup is equipped with an anti-siphon valve, make sure any replacement pickup has one, too.

Any modifications to fuel systems should be carried out by the dealer. This is a serious safety matter.

Flushing the Tank. Finally, while you've got the pickup unit removed, take a moment and look down into your fuel tank with a flashlight. See if there's any dirt or water building up down there. If there is, you might need to siphon the tank to clean out any contamination trapped inside. Also, when you reinstall the tank sending unit, you may have to replace the sealing gasket, depending on the type. When the unit's back in place, remember to check for fuel leakage next time you fill the tank, and correct any leaks immediately.

Portable-Tank Strainers. Portable tanks also are equipped with in-tank fuel strainers. If you see any contamination when you look into the tank's fill opening, then inspection of the strainer screen is warranted. You can get to the screen by unscrewing the mounting plate where your fuel hose attaches, and lifting the assembly up out of the tank.

Inspect the screen and clean it or replace it as needed. As with the permanent tank installations, the gasket sealing this assembly to the tank may have to be replaced once the unit is lifted out. Your dealer should be able to provide a new gasket or strainer screen. If dirt or water have contaminated the fuel and the inside of the tank, the fuel must be properly disposed of, and the tank flushed out until it is perfectly clean. Figure 7-2 shows the portable tank fuel strainer and pickup tube removed for inspection.

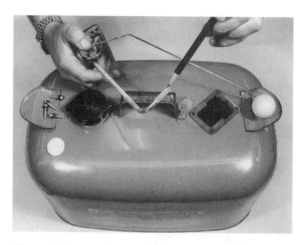

Figure 7-2. *A portable fuel tank strainer ready for inspection.*

The Fuel/Water Separator. Moving from fuel tanks to the next point in the fuel delivery system, you will usually find the spin-on fuel/water separator we discussed earlier in this chapter. Again, if your boat is not equipped with a water separator, I highly recommend that you add one. These filters are cheap insurance, and greatly ease maintenance problems. I've already explained the servicing of these units. The only additional recommendation I have regarding the filters is that it's a good idea to keep a spare element on board. Once they're full of water, these separators will generally stop fuel flow to the engine. Spinning on a new element can often spell the difference between motoring home under your own power and having to get a tow.

Incidentally, on large engines, or dual-engine installations, there may be an auxiliary electric "primer" pump installed between the tank and the fuel filter/water separator. Check with your dealer to see if your boat is equipped with one. Failure of this pump will cause fuel starvation and hard starting.

The Primer Bulb. The next stop in the fuel delivery system is the familiar primer bulb. This device is needed to start the draw of fuel from your tank, whether it's portable or built-in. The primer needs to fill the fuel system all the way to your engine-mounted fuel pump.

In addition to setting up this initial supply of fuel, the primer bulb serves one other important function that many people are unaware of. The bulb also has a one-way check valve built into it to allow fuel to flow toward the engine, but not back into the tank again. All primer bulbs have an arrow molded into them. This arrow must point toward the engine in the direction of fuel flow. Many engines have mysteriously stopped running simply because the fuel hose from the engine to the tank has been hooked up backward.

Whenever you replace fuel delivery hoses, or primer bulb/hose assemblies, make sure the inside diameters of the new hoses and fittings are the same as the old ones. The same principle applies to fuel filters added to your system—they must allow adequate fuel flow. Check the manufacturer's specifications. Failure to do so can cause trouble—poor engine performance at least; or severe engine damage, because of a lean fuel mixture, at worst.

Here are minimum inside diameters for fuel-delivery hoses and primer-bulb assemblies:

For engines above 150 hp, the recommended minimum ID is $\frac{3}{8}$ inch (10 mm). For engines of less than 150 hp, this is still the preferred diameter, but $\frac{5}{16}$ inch (8 mm) is acceptable.

Any metal pipe fittings in the system, such as those used at the spin-on fuel/water separator, must have a minimum inside diameter of $\frac{1}{4}$ inch (6.5 mm). The largest V8 models require a minimum inside diameter for these fittings of $\frac{9}{32}$ inch (7.1 mm). Always match whatever you have removed, assuming the installation was supplied by your dealer or engine manufacturer and has been giving no problems.

Fuel Pump Strainer. The next stop in the fuel line to your engine's carburetor is either an additional fuel strainer mounted separately under the engine cowl, or in some cases, a strainer built into the fuel pump itself. I prefer the separately mounted units as they often provide an additional visual clue to fuel quality.

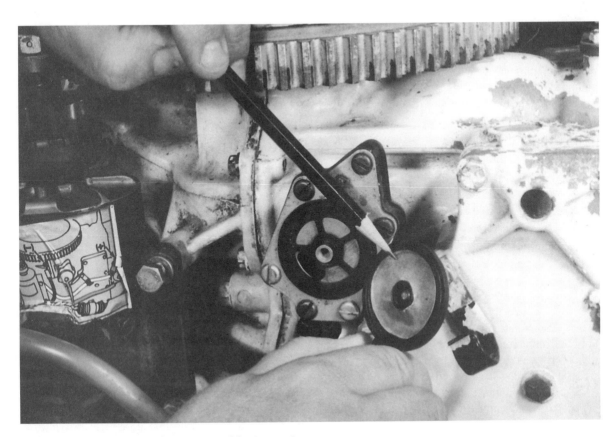

Figure 7-3. *A fuel pump strainer opened for inspection.*

Some pumps have a plastic cover that can be unscrewed, exposing a screen mesh designed as the final phase in your fuel filtration system. Whenever fuel delivery problems occur, this screen or remotely mounted strainer should be one of the first items checked. Figure 7-3 shows the built-in screen being checked for blockage. Check your owner's manual to see if your fuel pump has this feature.

Once fuel has passed through this final filter, it enters the fuel pump for delivery to the carburetor(s). But you don't need to bother about checking your carburetor(s) before you've done a thorough job of troubleshooting the fuel-supply system. More often than not, fuel-related problems crop up in the supply system rather than the carburetor(s). At the very least, the problems are always *generated* in the supply system, and sometimes affect the carburetor(s).

Fuel Supply Problems

Before you begin to tear your fuel system apart, it's a good idea to be able to recognize the symptoms of fuel system problems. It's also important to realize that these symptoms may be intermittent, which can further complicate the diagnostic process.

Here are the most common symptoms of trouble with the fuel supply:

- Loss of power.
- Engine "surging" at high speed.
- A "pinging" sound coming from the engine, caused by pre-ignition/detonation.
- Engine cutting out or hesitating on acceleration.
- General rough running.
- Engine quits, or simply won't start.

All of these problems result from one of your engine's basic needs not being met.

If you suspect you have a fuel delivery problem, start by disconnecting your fuel system from the engine. Attach a portable tank to the engine, one that is known to contain good fuel and to be in good working order. Run the engine and see if the symptoms go away. If so, then you can be certain you're on the right track. You can eliminate your carburetor(s) as a possible source of problems, and focus on the tanks, filters, and other parts of the delivery system.

If switching tanks makes no difference, it's possi-

ble that the running problem lies in the carburetor. In this event you'll need to sharpen your diagnostic skills a bit, and it won't hurt to apply some common sense either.

First, think about anything you may have done recently that may have created this new problem.

Did the symptoms develop shortly after filling with fuel? A sure clue.

Have you visually checked your fuel filters and water separators and found evidence of water or other fuel contamination? If the answer is yes, then it's a reasonable assumption that some of this water or dirt has got through the filters and fouled the carburetor.

Give your engine a quick look over. Any loose wires or corrosion evident, causing an ignition problem? When was the last time you changed the spark plugs? If the answer is at the proper interval as described in Chapter 3, then a bad spark plug is an unlikely cause for your present problem.

How old is your engine? If it's more than several years old, it is possible that gradual accumulation of dirt and gum deposits have finally settled in your carburetion system. Disassembly and cleaning will be required. That procedure is covered later in this chapter.

The Fuel Pump. A second way to isolate problems with the fuel system is to disconnect the fuel line that connects the engine-mounted fuel pump to the carburetor, and replace it with a clear piece of hose long enough to reach into a clean pail or coffee can.

Now, disable your ignition using one of the methods described in Chapter 5 of this book and use all the normal precautions associated with handling gasoline. Figure 7-4 shows fuel pump output being checked.

Once you've set up the hose and catch basin, crank the engine over or pull the starter cord at least five or six times. Observe the fuel as it flows through the clear hose. Look for any sign of water bubbles or rust particles. Also, see if any air bubbles are present. You should get a good solid flow of clear fuel. If dirt or water are showing up at this point in your fuel system, then not only will you have to eliminate the cause of that problem, but you'll most certainly have to remove the carburetor(s) for cleaning as well.

If air bubbles are present, several possibilities exist:

Figure 7-4. *Checking fuel pump output with a clear hose.*

1. You could simply be extremely low on fuel. (Presumably, though, you'll check the tank before you get to this point.)
2. You could have a loose fuel-line connection or a leaking hose somewhere in the delivery system, sucking in air.
3. You could have a problem with the fuel pump itself, causing air to be drawn into the system.

To test possibilities 2 and 3 above, you'll have to remove the clear hose and reinstall the original hose, replacing any clamps as needed.

Then, squeeze the primer bulb until it's firm, and hold pressure on it while looking for fuel leaks at the pump. If leaks are evident at the pump, you've identified the problem.

Other possibilities are a poor connection where the hose joins the engine, or where related hoses lead from

that point to the pump itself. If you find any, replace the hoses or clamps as required.

If no fuel squirts through the clear tube into your coffee can or pail when you're performing the output test, you'll need to verify that fuel is getting into the pump itself. This is easily done if you have a system with a separate strainer under the cowl, mounted before the pump. When you squeeze the primer bulb, you should see fuel flowing into the line feeding the pump. If this is evident, and the pump has no output when the engine is cranked over, the problem most likely lies in the pump itself.

If your engine has a strainer built into the pump, you'll have to remove the fuel hose to the pump and check for fuel flow at that point. Be careful when removing fuel hoses from these plastic pump assemblies; you must twist and pull simultaneously to avoid breaking the plastic nipple the hose fits over. To test for flow, squeeze the primer bulb with the hose disconnected and see if fuel comes out.

Checking the Seal.

Once you're certain that fuel is getting to the pump, but not leaving it when the engine is cranked, one possibility remains, and should be checked before you remove the pump. But first a bit of background.

Outboard-engine fuel pumps are driven by the positive and negative air pressure created by the piston's movements in the cylinder and the crankcase. Refer to Figure 1-4 to refresh your memory. This positive and negative pressure acts against a rubber diaphragm that spans a hole in the crankcase wall, making it "pant" back and forth. The moving diaphragm drives the fuel pump, which bolts directly over the orifice in the crankcase.

Some engines now have the pump mounted on a bracket under the cowl cover and connect the orifice to the pump via a small rubber hose. In either case, if the seal between the pump and the orifice is broken, then the pump won't work.

So, as a final check before removing the pump for overhaul, be sure the pump is screwed tightly to the side of the block, or make sure the connecting hose is in place and sealed tightly.

Fuel Pump Removal and Disassembly.

A faulty fuel pump should be removed from the engine, and carefully disassembled for inspection. Extreme caution is required here, as there are small springs and check-valves built into the pump assembly. Pay close attention to the location and orientation of each small part as you remove it from the pump assembly. Lay all the parts out on a clean piece of paper in correct sequence, to help reassembly.

Figure 7-5 shows the fuel pump being removed from the engine for disassembly and inspection. Figure 7-6 shows a disassembled fuel pump laid out in order of disassembly, ready for inspection and installation of an overhaul kit. Look for any accumulation of debris, cracks, holes, or deterioration in the rubber diaphragm inside the pump assembly. If you find any of these conditions, you've found your problem.

Fuel Delivery Step by Step

Before we move on to carburetor problems and solutions, we need to be quite sure we're feeding the carb with an adequate supply of clean fuel. Here's a final

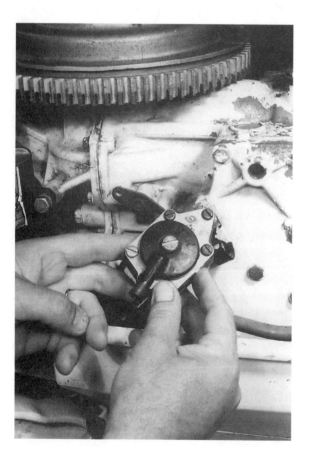

Figure 7-5. *Removing the fuel pump.*

Figure 7-6. *A fuel pump disassembled.*

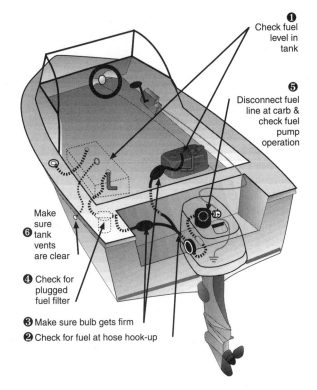

① Check fuel level in tank

⑤ Disconnect fuel line at carb & check fuel pump operation

Make sure ⑥ tank vents are clear

④ Check for plugged fuel filter

③ Make sure bulb gets firm
② Check for fuel at hose hook-up

Figure 7-7. *The fuel system—checking by numbers, for midsize and large engines.*

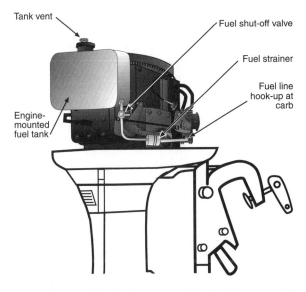

Tank vent

Fuel shut-off valve

Fuel strainer

Fuel line hook-up at carb

Engine-mounted fuel tank

Figure 7-8. *The fuel system—checks for a small engine.*

with an adequate supply of clean fuel. Here's a final check for you—the step-by-step systematic approach.

Figure 7-7 illustrates the fuel systems for midsize and large engines. The numbers give the order in which you should carry out your search for problems.

Figure 7-8 illustrates the check points for simple, built-in tank arrangements used on small engines.

Classic Symptoms of Carburetor Problems

After years of use, running without proper filtration, getting stuck with a really bad tank of fuel, or simple neglect, carburetor problems may plague you. If you have followed this chapter carefully, you should be able to make this determination with certainty.

For carburetor work you will need your engine workshop manual as well as this book. Carburetors vary widely, and internal design features are quite intricate. The essential components of all carburetors are the same however, and the principles of operation are the same for all. This means that basic symptoms of trouble are the same for all makes of carburetor, and you'll be able to identify them.

If the symptoms your engine is experiencing are the same as those listed above for fuel-delivery problems, and you have traced the contamination through the system and past the fuel pump, then quite simply, debris has reached the carburetor. You must remove the carburetor and clean it.

But symptoms of carburetor trouble may also pop up outside the carburetor itself. Flooding, a condition where too much fuel is entering the engine, or leaking out of the carburetor throat into the intake-air box, is a sure sign. Spark plugs that are wet with fuel, or black and sooty when removed, are a sign of too-rich a mixture.

Mixing Air and Fuel. The carburetor's job is to atomize fuel and mix it with air in a prescribed ratio. Too much fuel, or not enough air, alters this ratio and causes running problems. Fuel/air ratios must be maintained perfectly all the time the engine's running, from idle to maximum speed.

Lean conditions are especially dangerous. The mixture is lean when there is not enough fuel mixed with the air. Since the engine gets its lubrication from a mixture of oil and gasoline, inadequate fuel also means inadequate lubrication. At high speeds, a fuel mixture that's too lean can burn up a piston in short order.

Other carburetor problems may be revealed by a sudden onset of hard starting, especially when the engine is cold, indicating a problem with the choking or enrichment function of the carburetor.

Hesitation, or a surging, sputtering transition from low speed to high speed when you suddenly advance the throttle lever, is a sign of plugged jets inside the carburetor body.

Naturally, before you can isolate specific carburetor problems, you must understand the basics of how the carburetor works. The next section will give you the information you need.

How a Carburetor Works

Figure 7-9 illustrates the internal layout of a typical outboard engine carburetor. You'll note that carburetors contain a series of sub-systems that in technical lingo are referred to as "circuits." Each of these circuits carries out a specific job, and may operate only at certain engine speeds. Here's a description of each circuit, and its component parts:

The Float Circuit. The float circuit maintains the correct level of fuel in the float bowl. As fuel enters into the carburetor through the fuel inlet nipple, it continues through an internal passage to a needle valve.

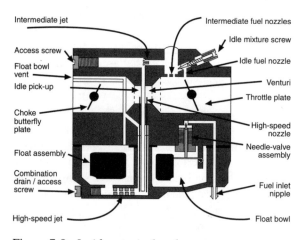

Intermediate jet
Access screw
Float bowl vent
Idle pick-up
Choke butterfly plate
Float assembly
Combination drain / access screw
High-speed jet

Intermediate fuel nozzles
Idle mixture screw
Idle fuel nozzle
Venturi
Throttle plate
High-speed nozzle
Needle-valve assembly
Fuel inlet nipple
Float bowl

Figure 7-9. *Inside a typical carburetor.*

This is the main "switch" turning the flow of fuel on and off. The needle valve is controlled by the float assembly.

As fuel runs past the needle valve into the float bowl, the rising float pushes the needle upward. When the float gets to the desired level, the needle completely closes the opening, shutting off the fuel supply. The maximum and minimum levels of the float are adjusted by bending the lever the float is attached to. It's actually the lever that makes contact with the needle. The terms used to describe these adjustments are "float height" and "float drop." These are the most critical adjustments to the inside of any carburetor, and should always be checked as part of carburetor service.

Floats stuck in either the open or closed position can be a problem. If the carburetor is flooding and gasoline seems to be pouring out, you likely have a float stuck open. A float stuck closed would be indicated by a "lean" condition, where insufficient fuel is getting to the cylinder(s). These problems usually occur after the engine has been in storage for extended periods, allowing the float valve needle to "freeze" from lack of use. Generally, several light taps on the side of the carburetor with a screw driver handle will free the needle valve.

The Idle Circuit. The idle circuit controls the amount of fuel entering the engine at idle speed only. It draws fuel up out of the float bowl and passes it through the idle pickup tube into the intermediate fuel chamber. The fuel passes the tip of the idle mixture screw, and is then pulled by vacuum through the idle fuel nozzle, located behind (downstream of) the throttle plate.

Adjusting the idle-mixture screw will alter the amount of fuel reaching the idle fuel nozzle, effectively changing the idle fuel/air ratio.

The Intermediate Circuit. The intermediate circuit controls fuel entering the system as the engine is accelerated, during the middle of the engine-speed range. As the throttle plate opens, it allows the intermediate fuel nozzles to be exposed to the engine vacuum located downstream of the throttle plate. The fuel is drawn to the intermediate nozzles through the same internal passages as the idle circuit, the difference being the position of the fuel nozzles relative to the throttle plate.

As the throttle plate continues to open, the volume of air passing through the carburetor venturi into the engine increases. This increased flow of air accelerates dramatically at the narrowest part of the venturi, where the high-speed fuel nozzle is located.

The High-Speed Circuit.
The high-speed circuit consists of the high-speed jet, located at the bottom of the float bowl, and the tube that connects the float bowl with the center of the venturi, sometimes referred to as the high-speed fuel nozzle. This tube will often surround the idle pickup tube, as illustrated in Figure 7-9.

This circuit works on a scientific principle called the "Bernoulli effect," named after Daniel Bernoulli, a Swiss mathematician who lived during the 1700s. Bernoulli's Law states that as air accelerates, a low-pressure area is created at the point of maximum acceleration.

The high-speed nozzle is located at the narrowest point in the carburetor "throat." There, because of the constricted passage, the air moves fastest and the pressure is lowest. In fact, the pressure is so low compared to the normal atmospheric pressure inside the float bowl that the effect is one of a vacuum drawing fuel from the float bowl up through this large-diameter, high-speed fuel nozzle. This comparatively high volume of fuel is mixed with the large amount of air being drawn into the engine to serve its high-speed fuel/air needs.

The Choke Circuit.
The final circuit incorporated into the outboard engine carburetor is the choke circuit, sometimes referred to as the primer or enrichment circuit.

When an engine is cold, it needs a richer fuel mixture to get started. Several methods are employed by manufacturers to accomplish this task.

The simplest, and most common, method is illustrated in Figure 7-9. With this system, the choke butterfly plate is closed during cold starting, restricting air flow into the carburetor throat.

The butterfly plate is activated by pulling a choke lever; on larger engines it may be activated by an electric solenoid switch. When you close this butterfly plate, you reduce the volume of air mixing with the fuel, effectively enriching the mixture.

Primer systems actually "squirt" an extra spray of fuel into the air stream. These primer systems can be activated by pulling a choke lever, as you would on a smaller engine, or by operating an electric solenoid valve on the larger engines. This valve opens an extra fuel nozzle in the carburetor, allowing a direct flow of fuel as you crank the engine.

An ingenious method used by Yamaha has a combination of a wax element (similar to a cooling-system thermostat) and an electrically activated heating coil to open and close an enrichment passage built into the carburetor body. This system has been widely used on the 1992 and newer Yamaha 9.9 hp four-stroke engines. The wax element screws directly into the top of the carburetor body. A cold engine makes it contract and pull the attached needle valve off its seat, opening the enrichment passage. That allows the normal engine vacuum to draw extra fuel directly from the float bowl. Once the engine starts, electric current from the engine's stator windings feeds the heating element, warming it and forcing it to expand. This pushes the needle valve closed and blocks the enrichment passage during normal engine operation. Figure 7-10 shows a cutaway of this thermal wax valve. If this system is in good working order, it is completely automatic, requiring no operator activation.

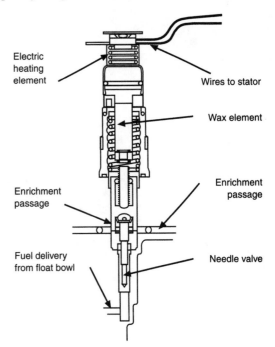

Figure 7-10. *Yamaha's thermal wax valve.*

Removing Your Carburetor

Removing your carburetor(s) for cleaning will involve disconnecting and removing a few other components first. Your workshop manual can help you here.

In all cases you'll have to remove the air box or breather assembly. Next, you'll have to disconnect the carburetor linkage, and often the choke mechanism will have to be taken off, too. On modern engines these components are frequently made of plastic, which has a tendency to become brittle with age and exposure to high engine temperatures. Be careful. Many of these parts snap together and frequently break when you snap them apart on disassembly. Pay close attention to the orientation of linkage arms and connecting links on multiple-carburetor engines; there is only one right way to reassemble these parts.

Once you've removed all the linkages and control pieces, disconnect the fuel line from the pump to the carburetor(s). Next, back off the nuts holding the carburetor to the engine. On smaller carburetors there will be two nuts for each carburetor. On larger, two-barrel carbs, such as those used on many V4 and V6 engines, there will be four nuts holding each carburetor in place.

Figure 7-11 shows a carburetor being removed for service. If your engine is equipped with more than one carburetor, it's a good idea to label each unit so it can go back in the exact same location. Now you're ready to begin evaluation of the unit before disassembly.

A common problem on older units is wear at the shaft that the main throttle plate is mounted on. An elongated hole wears in the body of the carburetor at the shaft's pivot points. Excessive wear at this point allows air to leak into the air/fuel mixture, causing leanness.

Figure 7-12 shows the point to check for this wear. Unfortunately, excessive wear here, indicated by no-

Figure 7-11. *Removing a carburetor.*

Figure 7-12. *Checking for throttle-shaft wear.*

ticeable side-to-side movement of the throttle shaft in the carburetor body, means the carburetor will have to be replaced. Rebuilding will be a waste of time. Check for wear at this point on any carburetor before you bother to disassemble it for cleaning. If you are in doubt about how much play is too much, take the carburetor to your dealer for appraisal. I can tell you from my experience that excessive play would be anything in excess of about 1/64 inch (0.4 mm). But it's hard to take an accurate measurement at this point, so the "feel" of an experienced mechanic is your best guide.

Disassembling Your Carburetor

Before disassembly starts, you should have on hand a rebuild kit for your carburetor as supplied by your dealer. These are often available as a "master" kit and a "clean-out" kit.

The clean-out kit generally consists of gaskets, O-rings, and a needle-valve assembly. Many kits also include a cardboard float gauge for checking its adjustment once you replace the needle-valve assembly.

Master kits will generally include all of those parts, plus such things as replacement idle-mixture screws, jets, a new float, and aluminum core plugs for the carburetor body. (These look like miniature "freeze plugs" for engines.)

In most cases, you will need only the "clean-out" kit. If your engine is old and has many hours on it, you may consider getting the master kit.

In addition to the parts kit, you will need an aerosol can of "Carb and Choke Cleaner," available at any auto parts store. You should also be sure to wear eye protection whenever spraying the carb cleaner. This stuff invariably ends up splashing back at you.

As a final precaution, lay out some clean paper to set all your carburetor parts on as you disassemble the unit. If you have multiple carbs, disassemble them one at a time. And take careful note: Never mix parts from one carburetor with another.

Once you've assembled all the necessary supplies, you can begin disassembly by unscrewing the float bowl from the main body of the carburetor.

With the float bowl removed, you can now get a pretty good idea of how badly the carburetor is gummed up by examining the contents of the bowl. Any contamination will have settled in the bottom of the bowl, and in many cases may have even partially solidified as a brown paste. If water contamination was your reason for getting to this point, you will actually see bubbles of water floating in the small amount of gas mixture left in the float bowl. You must remove all of this foreign matter and clean all the carburetor's internal passages and jets.

Begin by removing the float assembly. Push the small pivot pin that holds it in place out through the holder in the carburetor body. Be careful to follow any instructions given in your manual, as some of these pins are removed by pressing in one direction only.

Once the pin is pressed out, lift the float away from the carburetor. On some units, the needle will lift out of the needle-valve assembly as you remove the float. It will be attached by a small spring clip to the lever arm on the float. Once removed, the needle and spring clip will simply slide off the float lever. Next, get the appropriate hex socket or wrench and unthread the needle-valve body from the carburetor. The needle and seat assembly must always be replaced as a unit. Note: Some carburetor assemblies have a permanent seat that can't be removed from the carburetor body. In this case, the needle will be the only component replaced.

After removing the float and needle-valve assembly, you should carefully remove all traces of gaskets used in the carburetor assembly.

Leave the choke and main throttle plate in place. There is no reason to remove them. Just make sure they move freely and that the pivot shafts are not too loose in the carburetor body.

Be sure to remove any screws on side-cover plates, either plastic or metal, and lift the covers off. Removing the side plates and access screws will expose the small brass jets and calibrated orifices inside the carburetor passages.

For general cleaning, you shouldn't attempt to remove these jets with a conventional screwdriver even though they have a screw slot machined in them. They're designed to be removed with a special jet tool, and attempting to remove them will usually do more harm than good, raising small brass filings that can further plug the jets.

Once all the side covers, top covers, and access screws have been removed from the body of the carburetor, you can begin spraying with the carb and choke cleaner. Remember this solvent is quite strong, and prolonged exposure to the skin, or contact with your eyes is dangerous. Be aware that it will lift paint and destroy many rubber parts, so take precautions. Be sure to use the nozzle tube supplied with the cleaner to inject solvent into all small holes, jets, and passages inside the carburetor. Use the force of the aerosol spray to blow out any dirt or contamination.

Note: If your carburetor is quite dirty or old, it might be better to take the carburetor body to your dealer or local car repair shop and ask to have the body "dipped" in an extremely potent solvent tank designed especially for carburetor cleaning. This will remove stubborn deposits and spots you can't get to with aerosol spray.

Several precautions regarding these dip tanks are in order. First, remove all rubber or plastic components; the solvent will ruin them. Second, some manufacturers are epoxy-sealing the insides of carburetor bodies for corrosion protection; don't soak these parts for more than an hour or the solvent will attack the epoxy. Check your service manual for advice.

Sometimes you need to find the opposite end of the passageway you are blowing through and reverse the direction of flow with the cleaner nozzle. Spend some time on this to be certain all passages are clear.

When you're certain that all parts and passages are clean, wipe down the parts with a clean, lint-free rag. Any solvent residue will evaporate rapidly. Next, match the parts supplied in your rebuild kit with the components you removed from your carburetor. Don't be surprised to find an extra gasket or two in the kit—manufacturers often use one part number to service several carburetors. Be sure to match gaskets exactly, as sometimes they can be very close in appearance to one another. Often, one will block internal passageways, and not others; or vice versa. Rest assured, there is only one correct gasket in the kit.

The next step in the carburetor overhaul will be to install the new needle-valve assembly, and to adjust the float height and maximum drop. This is a critical step, as it is this adjustment that determines how much fuel will be maintained in the float bowl, ensuring correct delivery to the carburetor's venturi area.

Figures 7-13 and 7-14 show the float height and drop being checked with a standard machinist's ruler with a sliding T-bar set to the correct measurement. Your workshop manual will explain fully where to take these measurements. If you find your float measurements are different, adjust the float position by bending the metal lever and positioning tab until it agrees with the specifications.

Once the float is set properly, you can begin reinstalling the access screws you removed, and the top and side plates, replacing them with the parts provided in your carburetor kit. A precaution on reassembly is to be careful to tighten all screws evenly, starting from the center and working in a criss-cross pattern as you tighten. Also, and particularly with the newest carburetors that use many plastic components, remember that overtightening can be quite damaging, either dis-

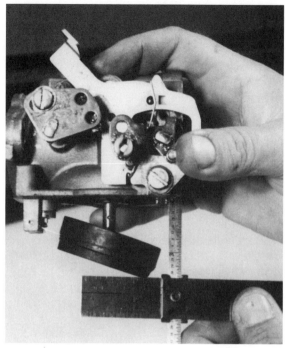

Figure 7-14. *Checking the float drop.*

Figure 7-13. *Checking the float height.*

torting the parts or, in extreme cases, actually breaking them. Snug is the operative word here.

Once you have your carburetor(s) cleaned and reassembled, install them on the engine using the new mounting gaskets provided in the rebuild/clean-out kits, and reattach all choke and throttle linkages.

If your engine has multiple carburetors, and you suspect that you changed any of the adjustments that synchronize the carbs, you must have the "synch and link" adjustments checked by your dealer.

If your engine has just one carburetor, your concern is that the idle mixture and speed are set correctly. These tasks are not especially difficult, but you must follow the manual for your specific engine, as there are just too many combinations to explain all of them here.

Choke and Primer Systems

If your engine has suddenly become difficult to start when cold, or is emitting excessive black smoke, running rough, or fouling plugs constantly, you may have a problem with the choke circuit.

On small engines, the manually activated systems that close a butterfly plate over the inlet end of the carburetor throat are quite easy to check by eye. You may have to remove an air-box cover installed on the engine, and turn or pull the choke lever on the engine control panel while observing the linkage and the butterfly plate in the carburetor throat.

If this plate is not closing and opening fully when the choke lever is moved, then the linkage problem will have to be corrected. Most often, all that's required is replacement of a small plastic or metal clip that has broken, allowing the linkage to fall out of place.

An engine with this butterfly plate stuck closed will run rich, and give off black smoke. The engine will run roughly and the plugs will become fouled. If the butterfly is stuck open, the engine will be difficult to start when cold.

Manual or electric primer systems are a little more difficult to diagnose, but will reveal the same symptoms as the manual butterfly systems. Black smoke indicates a rich mixture—the system is stuck on. Hard starting usually means the system is not functioning.

Further Checks.   For further checks on these systems, you'll need to get the engine running and allow it to warm up. Next, run the engine at about 2,000 rpm in neutral.

If you have a manual primer, push the primer knob three or four times and observe engine performance. If the primer is working, engine speed should decrease and the engine should begin to stumble and run poorly for a while before it clears itself. If not, the primer is not working.

With the electric system, push the key switch "in" several times to activate the primer solenoid. If the system is operational, the engine will stumble and lose speed. If not, the system is malfunctioning.

To proceed with further checks of the manual system, you must find out if the primer pump is a separate component, or if it's built into your carburetor. Your manual will have this information.

If the primer pump is separated from the carburetor, it will be connected to the carburetor by a small hose. To check it, squeeze the fuel-primer bulb at the fuel tank until it's firm. Then, disconnect the hose connecting the enrichment primer pump to the carburetor

and activate the primer knob on the engine. You should see fuel squirting from the hose. If not, look for a kink or some kind of restriction.

If the hose appears to be okay, the problem is in the primer pump assembly. Remove the unit from the engine and follow the instructions in your manual for disassembling and replacing any O-ring seals inside the pump. Note that these O-rings are often made of a special material designed to withstand fuel and additives—so use only dealer-supplied O-rings as replacements.

Once the O-rings have been replaced, reinstall the pump. It should now be squirting fuel just fine.

Manual Primers.   To check the operation of the built-in manual primers, you must get clear vision down the throat of the carburetor. Depending on the engine, this may mean removal of the air box. Once you can look down the carb throat, activate the primer knob. If no fuel builds up in the carb throat, the primer isn't working. You'll have to remove the carburetor and disassemble it.

Generally, these units have a diaphragm that acts against a spring inside the carb. Pushing against the diaphragm will force extra fuel into the carb throat. Most often, it's this diaphragm that ruptures. It will have to be replaced.

Electric Primers.   Electrically activated primer systems use a solenoid to move a plunger against a diaphragm in the primer-pump housing. The diaphragm displaces a calibrated amount of fuel into the carburetor throat, enriching the mixture.

These primers can fail electrically, or the diaphragm can rupture. There could also be a restriction in the delivery hose.

Other electric-choke systems use a solenoid to activate, via a lever and linkage, a series of choke butterflies.

In any case, checking the electric operation of the system is a matter of having someone operate the key primer switch in the remote-control box while you listen and feel for a light clicking noise coming from the solenoid.

The solenoid will be located near the carburetor linkage on the side of the engine block. Check your manual for the exact location. If necessary, use a screwdriver, as shown in Figure 4-1, to listen for the click of the solenoid engaging.

If you hear no sound when the switch is activated, then verify that the solenoid has a good ground to the engine block, and check for 12 volts at the wire coming from the remote control to the solenoid. Your engine manual's wiring diagram will pinpoint this wire for you. To check, simply set your multimeter to the DC volts scale and hook the meter's black lead to a good ground. Hook the red lead to the terminal connecting the wire from the remote-control box to the solenoid. With the key switch pushed in, you should have a reading of 12 volts.

If not, the problem may be in the plug assembly joining the engine to its main harness. If the connections inside this plug look good, you will have to trace this wire back to the remote control.

If no problems are found in this harness, the difficulty lies inside the remote-control box itself. You should send it to the dealer for repair.

If your test at the engine shows 12 volts getting to the solenoid, yet it's still not working, check the wire used as a ground lead. It should be securely held and making a good electrical connection. If you're satisfied that it is, then it's the solenoid that needs replacement.

If the choke/primer solenoid checks out okay, but is still not working properly, you'll need to investigate further.

Electric Chokes. In the case of an electrically activated butterfly-valve system, check just as you would for the manual system:

Remove the air box to expose the choke butterflies.

Activate the solenoid. When you hear it click, the butterfly plates should snap closed.

If they don't, the problem will lie in the linkage, and it should be quite obvious. Check and repair the linkage as needed.

With a solenoid-activated primer pump, the easiest and quickest way to check the pump is to remove the few screws holding the pump body to the solenoid and inspect for any blockage or a ruptured diaphragm. Use your engine manual as a guide. Clean or replace parts as needed.

Thermal Wax Valves. On the more advanced primer systems, such as Yamaha's thermal wax valve (see Figure 7-10), the symptoms of a malfunction are the same as for the other types.

If the problem is hard starting or stalling you'll

need to be certain the engine idle-speed adjustment is correct. If it's too low, the engine could stall. If it's too high, the engine vacuum will be reduced when you're cranking the starter motor, and the system will not draw in the extra fuel it needs.

If the idle speed is correct, remove the mounting screws for the thermal wax valve and pull it up out of the carburetor. Check the O-ring seal under the mounting flange for damage. If it's damaged, this is probably the cause.

Incidentally, on 1992 and early 1993 engines using this system, changes may be required to cure hard starting or stalling. Some thermal wax valves needed a modified jet to correct starting problems. Consult your dealer if your engine is of this vintage.

If your symptom is rough running or the emission of black smoke after engine warm-up, check the electric-heating element at the top of the thermal switch while the engine is running. It should be warm.

If it's not, it may not be getting voltage from the stator windings, or the electric coil inside the switch may be burned out.

To test the heating coil, use your ohmmeter. Trace the two black wires from the switch to their connection at the stator. Disconnect the wires. Use your ohmmeter and check for continuity through the electric heating coil. If you get a reading of between 4.8 and 7.2 ohms of resistance, the heating element is probably okay. To double-check this, take two of your alligator-clip jumper leads and clip them to the two wires from the thermal switch. Clamp one of the alligator leads to the positive post on your boat battery and the other to the negative. It doesn't matter which wire goes where. Watch the plunger on the thermo valve. If it begins to extend further from the valve housing, the heater is definitely working. In that case, your problem is with the stator windings on the engine. A dealer should be consulted.

Changing Technology. Regarding choking and priming systems in general, it's interesting to note that Yamaha alone used at least seven different methods for choking and priming between 1985 and 1995. Other manufacturers have used a wide variety of systems as well. It's obviously an area of constantly changing technology.

The systems described here are the most popular used during the last 20 years, but always use this book in conjunction with your engine's manual to help you solve problems with this important part of the fuel system.

Lubrication Systems

Over the years, manufacturers have tried various ways of mixing oil with the fuel on two-stroke outboard engines, not only to make refueling easier but also to provide more accurate fuel/oil ratios over the engine's entire operating range.

The truth is, an outboard engine doesn't need the same fuel/oil mix at low speed as it does at full throttle towing a water-skier. And a mixture that's too rich in oil results in excess exhaust smoke—an important challenge for outboard engineers to overcome.

There are currently several general types of lubrication for two-stroke engines, and one for four-stroke models. We'll take a look at all of these methods now, and I'll offer diagnostic and maintenance tips for each.

The Pre-Mix Method.

Mixing the engine lubrication oil with gasoline before use is by far the simplest method. Unfortunately, it's also the messiest and the greatest polluter of the environment.

Nothing complicated here, though. Just add the correct amount of oil to a certain volume of fuel in your tank, and the job is done.

One important consideration often overlooked is the grade of oil to use. I've said it before, but please stick to the current, state-of-the-art TCW-3. This blend has a far superior additive that promises to reduce many common outboard-engine problems such as sticking rings and carbon build-up in the combustion chamber.

It's also important to know what ratio of fuel to oil your engine maker recommends. In recent years, many manufacturers have reduced the ratio from 50 to 1 to 100 to 1. This means 100 parts of gasoline to 1 part of oil, or half as much oil as before—a significant change. Your owner's manual will give you the right ratio.

The order in which you do things counts, too. Remember to put the correct amount of oil in the tank *before* adding the gasoline, so the gasoline will mix with the oil as you fill the tank. The following chart gives the correct amount of oil to add for a certain volume of gasoline for each of the commonly used ratios:

Pre-Mix Oil Requirements

For each 3 gallons (11.4 liters) of gasoline add this amount of oil:

100 to 1 ratio: 4 fl. oz. (118 ml)
50 to 1: 8 fl. oz. (236 ml)
25 to 1: 16 fl. oz. (473 ml)

For each 6 gallons (22.7 liters) of gasoline add this amount of oil:

100 to 1 ratio: 8 fl. oz. (236 ml)
50 to 1: 16 fl. oz. (473 ml)
25 to 1: 32 fl. oz. (946 ml)

For each 18 gallons (68.1 liters) of gasoline add this amount of oil:

100 to 1 ratio: 24 fl. oz. (708 ml)
50 to 1: 48 fl. oz. (1.419 liters)
25 to 1: 96 fl. oz. (2.838 liters)

OMC's VRO System.

The Outboard Marine Corporation (OMC), which makes Evinrude and Johnson engines, uses a variable-ratio oiling (VRO) system for engine lubrication. Engines from 40 hp upward use this system today. The VRO system is unique among oil-injection systems. It delivers oil in varying fuel/oil ratios, based on the needs of the engine.

Like more conventional fuel pumps, this unit is powered by the positive and negative pressures inside the engine crankcase. The higher the engine speed, the more quickly the diaphragm in the fuel pump oscillates, pumping increased amounts of fuel.

Incidentally, the pump is bracket-mounted to the engine powerhead, and the crankcase pressure pulses are delivered through a connecting hose from the crankcase.

The VRO pump is fed oil from a separate reservoir with a capacity of 1.8 gallons (6.8 liters). You can order an optional unit holding 3 gallons (11.4 liters).

Built into the VRO pump is an electrical circuit to activate a warning horn if the supply system runs out of oil, or if the fuel delivery becomes restricted. Figure 7-15 gives the layout of hoses to the VRO pump.

Because of the critical nature of this pump, and the fact that some special tools are required for testing, I don't recommend that you try to service it. Let your dealer look at it immediately if you suspect trouble, to avoid expensive engine damage due to improper lubrication.

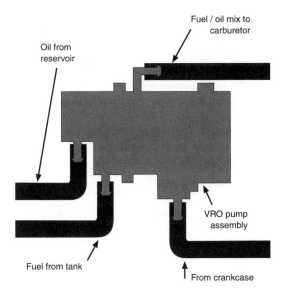

Figure 7-15. *Hoses attached to the VRO pump.*

Plastic tie-wraps or stainless screw-type clamps should never be used. The tie-wraps simply won't be tight enough, and the metal clamps may damage the hose.

The oil reservoir is one area you should check. First, and at least annually, remove the strainer screen from the tank and inspect it for tears or contamination. You'll need to buy a special #25 Torx screwdriver to remove the oil pickup cover plate on the tank. You can get one at any Sears or auto parts store.

Next, remove the four screws holding the fixture into the tank and lift the assembly up and out of the tank. Inspect the screen and clean it or replace it, as needed.

Figure 7-17 shows this screen removed for inspection. While you have the screen and the oil pickup assembly out of the way, remove the oil tank itself and thoroughly clean it out with a parts-cleaning solvent.

Since this system was first introduced in 1984 there have been at least nine changes in the VRO system's design. Many of these changes require a dealer retrofit to accommodate a new part or wiring harness. This kind of work obviously doesn't fall into the do-it-yourself realm.

You can, however, carry out routine checks of the system's filtration and warning systems. But let me warn you first that whenever you replace any hose clamps on the VRO system, you should use only the ratchet-style of clamp—see Figure 7-16. In use, the male and female ratchet pieces are squeezed together with a pair of pliers. It's important to note that these ratchet clamps often lose their grip after disassembly, and quite frequently need replacement.

Figure 7-16. *A ratchet-style hose clamp.*

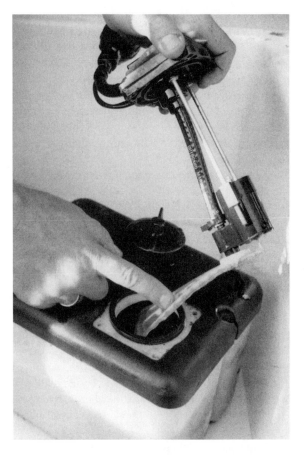

Figure 7-17. *Inspecting the oil reservoir filter screen.*

When you've cleaned the oil reservoir and serviced the strainer screen, take the opportunity to test the low-oil warning system. You can do this easily before you add oil to the tank.

With the boat's battery master switch on, turn the engine's ignition key on. With the oil reservoir empty, the warning horn should beep every 20 seconds. Now add oil to the reservoir and keep listening for the beep. When the tank is about one-quarter full, the beeping should stop.

A feature of 1996 and newer OMC engines—one that can be retro-fitted to many of the older units with VRO—is called the System Check warning system. This features a dash-mounted gauge and horn that is a great improvement over the earlier horn-only system. Previously, the horn had multiple functions, leaving you wondering what was malfunctioning when it sounded.

The System Check feature still gives an audible signal, but adds a row of very bright, light-emitting diodes (LEDs), visible even in bright sunlight, to pinpoint one of four possible causes for the sounding of the horn. As soon as the horn goes off, an LED flashes on the gauge unit to indicate one of four problems: no oil, overheating, low oil, or a restricted fuel supply. I can highly recommend this improved system because it costs far less than the repairs that could be associated with an unnoticed failure in any of these four crucial areas.

As with the VRO pump itself, I strongly recommended that if your warning system operation is suspect, you consult your dealer.

Mechanical Oil-Pump Systems. Other outboard engine manufacturers use a mechanically driven oil pump mounted on the engine block. It's connected to the throttle by way of a linkage arm.

The theory of operation here is that the crankshaft drives a gear in the pump, creating oil pressure. As the throttle lever is advanced to increase engine speed, the linkage arm also moves, opening a valve that allows more oil to flow into the oil pump.

There are two schools of thought on the matter of where to inject the oil, and this is where the significant difference lies between the mechanical oil-pump systems.

Yamaha, with its Precision Blend oil-injection system, injects the oil into a port in the carburetor-intake system behind the carburetor throttle plate. This means that only pure fuel passes through the carburetor. The oil blends with the incoming fuel/air mixture immediately after it leaves the carburetor throat, just before the mix enters the crankcase through the reed-valve plates. Yamaha engineers feel the pure gasoline mixture is less likely to gum up and form deposits inside the carburetor.

Mercury and other outboard makers inject the oil from the mechanical pump into a port in the engine-mounted fuel pump, where it is mixed with the fuel before it enters the carburetor. Figure 7-18 illustrates a typical mechanical injection-pump system, showing how all the major components are connected.

As with the VRO system, the mechanical-injection systems incorporate low-oil warning alarms that are also connected to an engine overheating sensor. Also, these systems (as well as the VRO) may have a built-in speed limiter. This sub-system is designed to reduce engine speed automatically when oil problems occur. This important feature goes a long way toward preventing severe engine damage in the event of an oil-

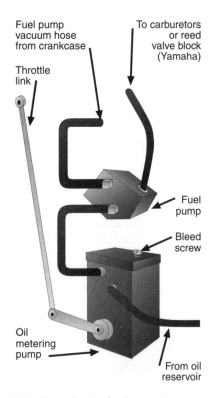

Figure 7-18. *A mechanical oil-injection system.*

injection problem. Check your owner's manual and study thoroughly the section describing warning-system tests and specific engine features such as the speed (rpm) limiter so you will know exactly what to do if one of these alarms sounds and your engine suddenly slows down mysteriously.

One problem with these systems can be air entering into the pump or oil lines. This can be caused if the system runs out of oil and becomes "air bound." Another problem that can stop oil delivery is a restriction in the vent hole at the top of the oil tank. The naturally oily surface at the fill cap attracts dirt and dust that can eventually block the air passage. This will cause a vacuum to develop within the tank. Since all of these systems on midsize engines have an engine-mounted oil reservoir set above the oil pump, they rely entirely on gravity to get the oil to the pump. Gravity, however, won't overcome a vacuum. Periodically check the tank vent, and clean it as needed.

If you do run out of oil, or if you find the tank vent was plugged, you may have to bleed air from the pump before you run the engine again. Mercury engines have a bleeder screw on their pumps at the top of the assembly. Figure 7-19 shows the location of the pump and bleeder screw on 75-hp Mercury outboard.

Bleeding the pump is an easy task, although a little messy. First make sure the oil tank is full. Next, get a rag and place it under the oil-pump to catch oil that will leak out of the air-bleed screw.

With the engine not running, open the bleeder screw three or four turns. Let the oil drip out of the bleed screw until no air bubbles are visible. Once you have a good flow of oil at this point, snug the bleed screw back up, and wipe spilled oil off the pump and surrounding area.

Next, run the engine at idle and observe the oil as it leaves the pump through the clear delivery hose connected to the fuel pump. You may see some air bubbles at first, but these should clear out in a few minutes, showing a solid stream of oil going through the hose. Never attempt to run the engine at high speed if you can see air bubbles in this hose. As with the VRO system, it's not recommended that you try to adjust or rebuild any of the components in these systems. Calibration requires special tools in some cases and a solid mechanical background to ensure that oil delivery is correct at all engine speeds.

If you ever suspect that your oil delivery system is

Figure 7-19. *The oil-injection pump bleeder screw on a 75-hp Mercury.*

malfunctioning, either because the warning horn has sounded, or because of excessive blue smoke in the exhaust, there's a simple trick that will protect your engine from damage.

First, if an alarm has sounded, make sure the cause is not overheating. Look for water squirting from the tracer hole on the side of the engine. That tells you the water pump is working. Your owner's manual might be helpful here, too, allowing you to distinguish between overheating and an oil system problem.

Once you are sure the problem is related to the oil-injection system, and not from overheating, you can set up an alternate fuel/oil system. Simply disconnect the fuel inlet to your engine and install a portable fuel tank with oil pre-mixed at a 50 to 1 ratio. This will ensure that your engine is adequately lubricated until you can get to a dealer.

In summation, if you are mechanically inclined and have a reasonable amount of experience, it's possible to run through the oil-injection system checks outlined in workshop manuals and fix any problem that may come up with these systems. But if you are unsure of yourself, stay away until you've gained more experience. Stick to the routine maintenance tasks, such as cleaning the tank, checking the oil-strainer screen, and clearing tank vents. Follow the routine to make sure your alarm system is functioning as it should be.

Keeping this system clean, and being sure that all hose and wiring connections are tight, will give you years of trouble-free service.

Oil Recirculation Systems.   All outboard engines since 1969 are equipped with a system that's designed to recycle excess oil accumulating in the crankcase. Oil that's injected into the engine will not be completely consumed as it enters the combustion chamber with the fuel-and-air mix. Some of it "puddles" inside the crankcase.

To remove this excess oil, manufacturers have devised a simple system of small fittings screwed directly into the side of the powerhead block assembly at key points. These fittings have hoses connected to the carburetor intake system, so the excess oil from the crankcase can be mixed with the incoming air/fuel mixture.

This system is extremely simple and virtually trouble-free—but it can cause trouble if a hose becomes cracked or disconnected at either end. If your engine is equipped with this system, your workshop manual will have a detailed routing diagram showing where all hoses connect. Follow this diagram closely to ensure that all connections are correct.

Classic symptoms of trouble with this system would be excessive oil accumulation on the outside of the engine block, or a rough idle condition.

If a hose for this system becomes disconnected, you will have opened a small hole directly into the crankcase. Air entering the crankcase, or the carburetor intake for that particular cylinder, will effectively lean out the fuel/air mix. Of course, if you have religiously followed maintenance instructions in this book and have periodically checked all hose connections on your engine, this should never be a problem.

Four-Stroke Engine Lubrication.   If you have a four-stroke outboard engine, its lubrication system is entirely different from the two-stroke systems we've talked about so far.

You'll never have to worry about mixing oil with fuel. You'll never wonder if your oil-injection system is functioning. Four-strokes don't have or need any oil mixed with the fuel.

The four-stroke lubrication system is quite similar to the one in your car engine. It's a pressurized system with a conventional oil pump that lubricates key points inside the engine crankcase. Your engine will have either a strainer or, as on some of the newer Honda and OMC products, a conventional spin-on oil filter element—just like the one on your car. Figure 1-2 in Chapter 1 shows the location of the oil sump and the oil pump itself.

There are no user-serviceable components within these systems, other than a filter or strainer that must be serviced at prescribed intervals described in Chapter 3 of this book.

As all the working components of the oil pump are constantly submerged in lubricating oil, the internal parts of this system will last as long as the engine itself. The only things that can damage a pressurized system of this type are running without oil or running beyond the recommended oil-change frequency, which may cause a build-up of varnish and sludge that can block oil-delivery passages.

In addition to oil and filter changes, simply check the oil-pressure warning system on your particular engine following the instructions in your owner's manual each time you use your engine, and check the oil level as part of your daily checklist. If ever you have reason to believe that your oil pressure is inadequate, even when the engine's properly filled with the correct oil, consult your dealer immediately.

Chapter 8

Servicing the Steering and Trim Systems

Boats with outboard motors are generally steered in one of three ways. Small boats are controlled by a tiller handle on the motor. Midsize boats usually have a steering system controlled by cables. And large boats mostly employ hydraulically assisted power steering.

Whichever system you have, remember that steering control for the boat begins at the tiller handle or steering wheel, and ends under water at the trim tab mounted on the engine.

The condition of your boat's underwater hull may affect steering noticeably. Uneven loading of your boat can have the same effect. Be sure these aren't the problems before you start blaming the steering system.

Tiller Steering

Tiller steering is the simplest of all systems with the fewest moving parts. All steering components are mounted directly on the engine itself, and quickly checked.

If looseness is evident in this system, check the point where the tiller handle hinges upward, and be sure the engine itself is securely mounted to the boat. Tighten the hinge pivot bolt if need be. You should be checking the mounting screws as part of your daily

routine, but if you've been negligent, inspect them at the first sign of steering looseness.

If your steering gets too tight, the problem is a lack of lubrication of the steering-pivot bushings, as shown in Figure 3-5 on page 11. Once lack of lubrication makes the steering begin to seize, you may have to spend some time pumping in new grease and working the tiller back and forth to free up the mechanism. So again, sticking to the routine maintenance schedule outlined in this book will save you time and effort in the long run.

Steering-Tension Adjustment. Most smaller engines have a steering-tension adjustment built into the steering pivot tube. Often this adjuster is identified as a slotted screw with a tensioning spring under it screwing directly into the side of the pivot tube. Some new engines even have a lever mounted on the engine console to adjust the steering tension. Check your owner's manual for the exact location of this adjustment on your engine. It is important to remember that this adjustment should never be tightened to the point where resistance to the steering is felt. This adjustment is not intended to be an adjustable autopilot.

Trim Tab Adjustment. A common problem with tiller steering is a strong pull on the tiller handle at medium-to-high speed. This strain, and your constant effort to hold the boat on a straight track, can be extremely tiring to your steering arm. This problem can be easily corrected with an adjustment to the trim tab, but may require a trial-and-error procedure to get perfect results.

First make sure the problem isn't being caused by an uneven load in the boat. In a small boat, weight positioning is critical, so any imbalance that causes the boat to lean to one side or the other, or dip the bow or stern sections while it's at rest, will definitely affect steering underway. Don't forget that *your* body weight counts as well. You may want to position some heavier objects opposite your normal seating position to keep the boat from listing when you're underway.

Also be certain that your steering pull isn't caused by excessive, uneven sea growth on your boat's bottom. If you trailer your boat, this shouldn't be a problem but if you leave the boat in the water for extended periods, and especially for extended periods with little or no use, this could be the cause. The boat will have to be hauled and the bottom cleaned.

Once you are certain that uneven weight distribution or excessive sea growth is not the cause of your steering problem, there is only one more item to check and that's the adjustment of the trim tab on your engine.

Figure 8-1 is a fish-eye view of the trim tab, looking straight up from below. Note the reference scale used when adjusting it. Very small changes to this adjustment make very big differences in a boat's ten-

dency to pull to one side or the other, so don't be heavy-handed here.

To adjust the trim tab, simply loosen the bolt in the center, move the tab in the desired direction, and retighten the bolt. On some engines, the bolt actually comes down through the top of the lower engine leg, and may have a round plastic cap covering it.

If your boat is tending to steer to starboard (the right) when you leave the tiller alone, you must adjust the trim tab so that its front (leading) edge is aimed slightly to port (the left).

Make adjustments in small increments and try the boat out with a normal load to check for improvement. Adjust the tab until the tiller on the engine points straight while underway, with minimal effort needed to hold the boat on a straight track.

If your boat tends to pull to port (left) while underway, adjust the trim tab so that its leading edge is pointing slightly to starboard with the engine in the straight-ahead position. In addition to trim tab adjustments, trim in the fore-and-aft plane might also affect steering. Trim angle should be adjusted so the boat rides level, or with the bow pointing slightly up when underway with a normal load. (See discussion on adjusting trim later in this chapter.) By making careful adjustments in small increments, you will be able to achieve a nearly neutral helm with no pulling at all.

Small engines of 6 hp or less often have a non-adjustable skeg that is actually the exhaust outlet, so there is nothing to adjust on them. Luckily, steering is generally not a problem with these low-powered engines.

Cable-Controlled Steering

The most common steering system after the tiller is the single-cable control. Depending on the size of your engine or engines, a dual-cable installation may be used. Figure 8-2 shows possible single- and dual-cable layouts.

These cable systems use either a rotary-style steering "head" or a rack-and-pinion arrangement in which a heavy "spring" is wrapped around the inner core of the cable. The coils of this "spring" mesh with a gear inside the steering head. Teleflex refers to this as a helically wound cable and in fact the spring acts as a helical gear.

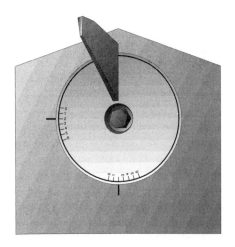

Figure 8-1. *Typical engine trim tab, showing adjustment scale.*

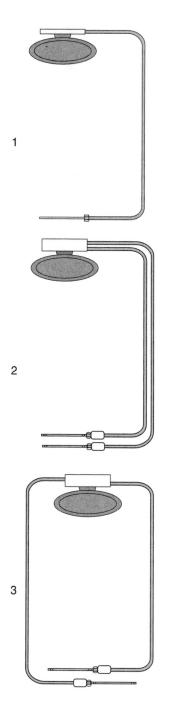

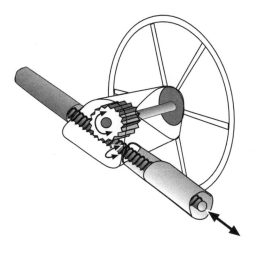

Figure 8-3. *How a rack-and-pinion system works.*

Figure 8-2. *Possible single-cable and dual-cable steering systems.*

In the rotary system, as the steering wheel is turned, a gear either pushes or pulls the spiral mechanism on the steering cable. This force either pushes or pulls the steering cable inside its sheath, effectively extending or shortening its length at the point where the cable attaches to the outboard engine. Figure 8-3 shows how the rack-and-pinion is arranged inside the steering head, and how the gear and cable work in unison.

Problems with these systems often occur at the engine end of the system, in the area most exposed to the weather. If you don't respond to the symptom of tight steering, you can expect damage to the steering-head mechanism that will ultimately ruin it. If you catch them early, most problems can be corrected right at the engine, with no need to replace expensive parts. The steering head is generally factory-sealed and requires no field servicing.

The biggest trouble spot on these cables is the point where they enter and go through the tilt tube on the engine. Figure 8-4 shows a steering cable being removed from the tilt tube in a typical installation.

If the inside of this tube and the end of the steering cable are not well lubricated, seizure will occur here, making the steering wheel very hard to turn and causing premature failure of the steering head. So, lubrication at this point is critical if you want trouble-free operation and a long-lasting steering system.

The main problem with these tilt tubes is that, until just recently, they've been made of mild steel. Sure, the outside of the case is painted—but the inside isn't. If

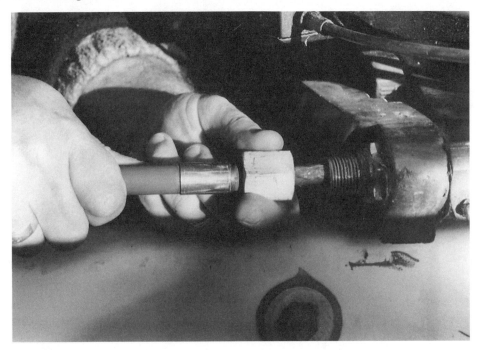

Figure 8-4. *Removing a steering cable from the tilt tube.*

there's no grease in the tube, it will rust solidly to the steering cable.

If your steering has begun to seize, it's a good idea to remove the steering cable, as shown in Figure 8-4, and thoroughly clean the inside of this tube and the extended length of the steering cable itself. On most boats, however, there is one problem with this procedure: the engine might have to be unbolted from the transom and either lifted from the transom while the cable is slid from the tilt tube, or slid along the edge of the transom away from the cable to provide enough room to slide the cable completely out of the tube. If you have to do this, make sure to get the right lifting equipment and a helper—a typical 100-hp outboard weighs around 300 to 350 pounds (140 kilograms).

The odds are good that the inside of the tilt tube will be rusted, but you can make a tool to clean out all the rust and dried-up grease. See Figure 8-5.

Use wet-and-dry sandpaper of 100 or 200 grit, folded to expose grit on both sides, in one end of the rod, and fit the other end into an electric drill. Run the

drill at medium speed and spray generous amounts of WD-40 or the like into the steering tube as you work the tool in and out. Depending on how badly the inside of the tilt tube is gummed-up, you may have to change the sandpaper several times, because it clogs with the dried grease and rust. Use the same wet-and-dry paper with WD-40 to clean the steering-cable extension.

Once you've removed all the old grease and rust from the tilt tube and cable, coat both the inside of the tilt tube and the outside of the cable with a waterproof grease recommended by your engine manufacturer, and reassemble the steering mechanism.

Remember to use a new self-locking nut where the cable joins the steering link or arm on the engine. See Figure 8-6.

If you don't have a new nut, apply some thread-locking compound, such as Loctite, to the threads inside the nut before reinstalling it. Remember, this single nut and bolt is the final link between you and your engine in the steering system. If this nut and bolt vibrate loose, you'll suddenly feel excessive play in the

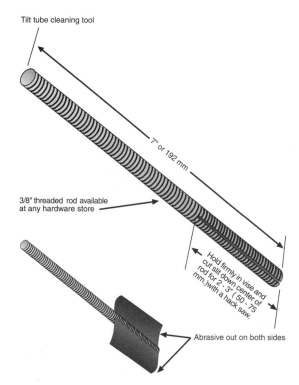

Tilt tube cleaning tool

7" or 192 mm

3/8" threaded rod available at any hardware store

Hold firmly in vise and cut slit down center of rod for 2 - 3" (50 - 75 mm.)with a hack saw.

Abrasive out on both sides

Figure 8-5. *Tilt tube cleaning tool.*

steering, and if the bolt falls out completely, you'll lose all steering control.

Naturally, if you've followed all the recommended daily, monthly, and seasonal service procedures, you will rarely experience steering problems—only after many years of use, when parts of the system just naturally wear out.

Measuring for a New Steering Cable.

Eventually, you'll have to replace the steering cable on your boat. Sooner or later, sun and salt will take their toll on the cable's outer sheathing, or the lubrication inside the sealed unit will dry up and make steering difficult.

Measuring for proper length is important. A cable that's too short will cause the steering to bind. A cable that's too long can make the steering too sloppy. Figure 8-7 shows the key measurements you'll need to take.

Simply add distance 1 + 2 + 3. If your cable runs through the tilt tube on your engine, add 6 inches (152 mm) to your 1 + 2 + 3 measurement to get the total cable length needed. If your cable mounts to a bracket (as shown) on either the transom or in the motor

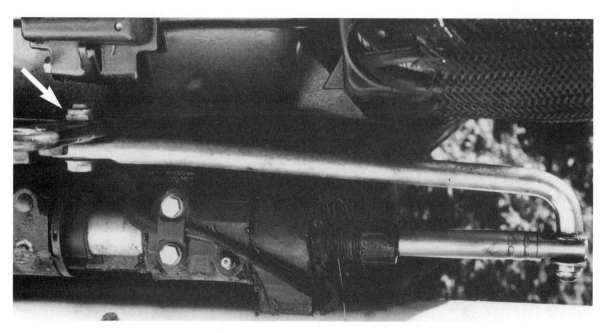

Figure 8-6. *Steering-link arm nut and bolt.*

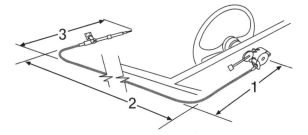

Figure 8-7. *Key measurements for a steering cable.*

splashwell, subtract 6 inches from your 1 + 2 + 3 measurement to get the cable length you need.

Once the length is established, any good marine supply store can provide a quality replacement from either Teleflex or Morse controls, the two most common makers.

To install the new cable, follow the instructions that come with it. This is not a particularly difficult task—just remember the precautions mentioned here.

Hydraulic Steering

Hydraulic steering systems use fluid pressure to transfer the motion from your steering wheel to the motor. The steering cable is replaced by pipes containing the hydraulic oil. As you turn the steering wheel to port or starboard, a valve in the steering head is activated, causing the hydraulic oil to push on one side or the other of a two-way hydraulic ram mounted on your engine.

Hydraulic systems give a mechanical advantage that makes it less of an effort to steer large, more powerful boats equipped with outboard engines. These systems are generally quite trouble-free and require very little service or maintenance. Figure 8-8 shows a typical single-engine, "side mount" hydraulic-steering system.

The most popular of these systems is manufactured by Teleflex Inc. It's called the SeaStar system, and consists of a helm with a hydraulic pump, two connecting hoses, a hydraulic ram, and the hardware for fixing the ram cylinder to the engine.

You add oil to this system through a fill port at the top of the helm unit. Be sure to use nothing but the specified hydraulic fluid because the wrong stuff can cause steering malfunction and damage the system.

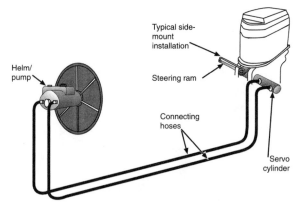

Figure 8-8. *A typical "side mount" hydraulic system.*

These are the recommended fluids:

> SeaStar oil (part number HA5430)
> Shell Aero Fluid #4
> Esso Univis N15 or J13
> Texaco HO15
> Chevron Aviation Hydraulic Fluid A
> Mobil Aero HFA
> Petro Canada Harmony HV115—in Canada only

You need to watch two things on hydraulic systems. First, when you add fluid, or remove and reinstall hydraulic hoses and fittings, the surrounding area must be totally clean. Hydraulic pumps are machined to extremely close tolerances and incorporate intricate valving to create high pressure. Even the smallest particle of dirt, or the lint from a cloth rag, can block the hydraulic circuits inside the pump or ram.

Second, you should know that these systems operate at pressures of as much as 1,500 pounds per square inch (psi), or a little over 100 bars. Never use any hoses or fittings not designed to handle pressures this high. It can be dangerous, and cause spongy steering at least—total loss of steering at worst.

Another thing—never attempt to shorten a hose by cutting a fitting off and getting a hydraulic shop to swage a new one on. These hoses are available from Teleflex in lengths of 2 feet (61 cm) to 40 feet (12.2 m). My advice is to get the factory-approved hose. Your steering is just too important to take any chances with.

Routine Servicing. Routine servicing of the hydraulic steering system consists of visual checks for any sign of hydraulic-fluid seepage at the helm pump and the ram cylinder. Periodically, you should check the hoses connecting the helm to the ram for any sign of chafing or cracking of the outer sheath. These hoses must be properly secured to minimize flexing and movement when they're under pressure. Excess movement will cause a spongy feeling in your steering wheel. At any sign of chafing or outer sheath cracking, you should replace the faulty hose as soon as possible.

In terms of maintenance, it's a good idea to check the tightness of the hose fittings at the back of the helm pump and at the servo ram on the engine as part of annual servicing. Also, you should keep the polished ram at the engine end clean and free of dirt. Wipe it down with a clean cloth periodically. Any dirt on this ram will be drawn into the ram cylinder as the piston retracts and will eventually damage the lip seal inside the cylinder, causing a fluid leak.

Symptoms of Problems. Problem symptoms for these systems can be narrowed down to two primary areas. Any excessive noise from the system can mean air has somehow entered the works. Spongy steering or steering that "skips" is another indicator of air in the system.

To correct this, check all fittings and connections, snugging them up as required. Air doesn't just enter the system without reason; there must be a leak somewhere. If you're lucky, it will be simply a loose hose connection. If you find no leaks at the hose hook-ups, check the area just behind the steering wheel where the steering shaft exits the helm/pump for any evidence of hydraulic fluid. If none is present, you can proceed.

If a leak is present at this point, the helm will have to be removed and brought into a dealer for replacement of the shaft seal. Removal is easily done by undoing the four nuts that hold the helm/pump to the dash console and disconnecting the hose lines. Be sure to cap, or to protect in some way, any exposed hose ends or pump hook-up fittings. You don't want dirt to enter the hoses or the hydraulic circuitry.

Check the hydraulic ram at the engine. If oil is accumulating on the polished shaft, the cylinder seal is leaking, and it will have to be removed and taken to your dealer for an overhaul. These components actually have an extremely low failure rate and rarely need any overhaul work.

Once you've fixed any leaks, either by tightening the connections or overhauling the hydraulic components, you can add fluid through the filler port at the top of the helm/pump.

Bleeding a Hydraulic System. If any part of the hydraulic steering system is removed for resealing or replacing a part, some air will enter the system. You'll need to bleed it out.

This is very easy to do, but you need patience. It could take as long as a half-hour to purge all the air from the system, depending on how much entered.

Figure 8-9 shows the direction of oil flow through the system when you turn the steering wheel clockwise. (Oil flow through the system will be in the opposite direction when you turn the wheel in a counterclockwise direction.)

The ram cylinder on these systems will generally have a bleeder screw built into the fitting where the port and starboard hydraulic hoses attach to the cylinder. If not, the system can be bled by loosening the hose fitting slightly and then tightening it as you bleed the system.

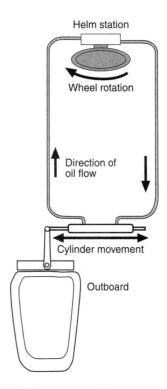

Figure 8-9. *Direction of oil flow through the hydraulic system.*

Start the bleeding process by topping up the oil reservoir in the helm pump. Next, crack the bleeder screw or hose fitting at the ram cylinder for the starboard pressure hose as shown in Figure 8-8. Turn the top of the steering wheel slowly as far as it will go to the right (starboard). Close the bleed screw or tighten the hose fitting.

Now crack the bleed screw or hose fitting line for the port pressure hose at the ram cylinder. Slowly turn the top of the wheel all the way to the left (port). Close the screw or tighten the hose fitting.

Check the fluid level in the helm reservoir, topping up as needed.

Repeat these steps until only fluid begins to leak from the bleed screws or hose fittings and there is no evidence of air bubbles.

Then tighten the connections, wipe away any spilled fluid, and give the reservoir a final top-up. Your system is now ready for service.

Trim and Tilt Systems

Your engine will have either a manually adjustable trim and tilt mechanism, or an electrically activated hydraulic system, depending on how big it is.

The tilt feature allows you to raise the lower unit of the engine out of the water when it's not in use.

The trim feature and adjusts your boat's "trim" (her floating attitude in a fore-and-aft plane) while you're underway. It helps start the boat planing, and adjusts the boat's handling characteristics in differing sea conditions.

Once again, however, there are no parts of this system that you can service in the field. Nevertheless, you can and should attend to the maintenance routine. You can also service the electric control circuit in these systems.

To understand the purpose of the trim and tilt system, it helps to break the term into its two components.

"Tilt" is easy: This simply refers to lifting the motor all the way to its limit in the "up" position. This gets the lower unit out of the water when the boat is not in use, and enables you to trailer the boat without having the engine hit the road.

Almost all engines have a trailer-lock mechanism built into this linkage that is designed to relieve strain on the hydraulic system as you bounce down the highway. A lever activates a mechanical locking device

under the mounting bracket. Check the lever for free movement periodically, and lubricate the locking device along with the rest of the tilt-mechanism pivot points, as shown in Figure 8-10.

Check your engine owner's manual to be sure you know how this mechanism works on your specific engine, as there are some variations in design from one manufacturer to another.

"Trim" relates to the need to have the motor perpendicular to the water as the boat moves at high speed. With a manual system, the trim is adjusted at the dock by moving the lock pin in the series of holes on your mounting bracket. Trial and error is required here, and it's important to load the boat normally to make the adjustments.

Figure 8-11 shows a motor with too much "in" trim, that is, the propeller is too far "in" toward the transom.

Figure 8-12 shows what happens when the motor has too much "out" trim, that is, the propeller is too far out from the transom.

Figure 8-13 shows a boat and motor trimmed correctly. But unusual weight in the bow will alter the set-

Figure 8-10. *Lubrication points on a manual tilt mechanism.*

Figure 8-11. *Boat and motor with too much "in" trim.*

Figure 8-12. *Boat and motor with too much "out" trim.*

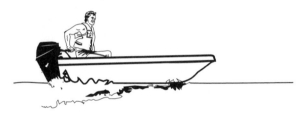

Figure 8-13. *Boat and motor with correct trim.*

ting, of course, forcing the bow downward. This "bow down" condition can also be a factor in creating excessive steering pull to one side or the other. Likewise, too much weight toward the stern will raise the bow abnormally high and cause the steering to feel dangerously "loose."

A good starting point is to set the lock pin in the second set of holes from the full "in" position. Run the boat and see how it trims out at speed. If the bow seems to be down, forcing the boat to plow through the water, move the locking pin "out" one hole and try again. This also affects steering pull. If the bow is up in the air, move the pin "in" one hole and try again. Don't try to make these adjustments while you're underway, of course.

Once you find the correct setting, you'll generally leave the pin in place permanently, unless you need to make adjustments for extreme loads.

Electric/hydraulic trim systems have a distinct advantage over their manual counterparts because you can adjust the trim angle as you move through the water, achieving the best trim angle for the speed of the boat and varying load situations.

Electric trim systems all work much the same way. They're activated by an electric switch on your instrument console or in the handle of the remote-control lever. This switch triggers one of two relays mounted on the engine, one for "up" and one for "down." Sometimes, too, there is a master control relay.

The relays send current to an electric motor on your engine-mounting bracket. The motor can run in two directions, and operates a pump that hydraulically moves a piston or pistons on the engine-mounting bracket.

The piston and the electric motor are mounted on a heavy metal "block" that contains a series of hydraulic control valves. They perform all kinds of functions, including relieving high pressure, control of the motor in the event it strikes an underwater object, and control of the engine's tendency to lift out of the water when it's in reverse gear. The valves also direct hydraulic fluid for the up-and-down functions of the hydraulic cylinders.

In addition, the valve bodies have a manually activated pressure-relief control to bypass the whole system in the event of a mechanical or electrical failure that would otherwise make it impossible to raise or lower the engine. This allows you to tilt the engine all the way up to the "trailer lock" position until a repair can be made.

Figure 8-14 shows a typical trim motor and cylinder assembly on the mounting bracket of a midsize outboard engine. The key maintenance and troubleshooting points are indicated by the arrows in the picture.

Figure 8-15 shows a typical manual bypass screw on a midsize Mercury outboard engine.

Problems with these assemblies are related to their locations. The electric trim motor is mounted right at the waterline on the bracket. It constantly gets splashed with water. Exposed wiring, and trim-limiting and indicator switches are also in the same vicinity. On some units, exposed hydraulic lines are often encrusted with barnacles, as are the hydraulic cylinders and their mounting pads.

Walk down any dock where outboard-powered boats tie up and you'll see the effects of the rough environment this equipment spends its life in. Rust,

Figure 8-14. *Typical hydraulic trim and tilt mechanism.*

Figure 8-15. *Hydraulic bypass screw on a midsize outboard.*

corrosion, and eventual component failure from water entering the electrics, and in extreme cases the hydraulics, of this system are the most common problems.

All the same, maintenance here is simple. It boils down to keeping all these components as clean and rust-free as possible. At the first sign of rust, or paint bubbling, the affected area should be scraped, primed, and repainted. The procedures are given in Chapter 10 of this book.

Hydraulic problems are rare with these systems. Since the system is totally sealed, and essentially self-contained, there's not much to go wrong. You don't have to change the hydraulic fluid but manufacturers do recommend that you check the fluid level seasonally. In reality, if there have been no signs of leakage, and the system is functioning normally, even this is not really necessary, as there is no place for the fluid to go.

Opening up the system to check the fluid level can actually do more harm than good, as the smallest particle of dirt or even a paint chip can enter the system

through the fill cap and cause one of the internal hydraulic valves to malfunction. If you feel you must perform this check, be certain to thoroughly clean the filler cap and surrounding area and make sure the engine is in the tilt-up position with the trailer lock engaged before you remove the plug.

Figure 8-16 shows the filler cap on a typical midsize Mercury engine. These systems generally use a proprietary hydraulic fluid supplied by your dealer, but a suitable substitute is Dexron automatic transmission fluid, as used in cars. Check your owner's manual to be certain of the correct oil for your system.

After years of use, the seals on the hydraulic cylinders of your trim and tilt system may begin to leak. You'll see red oil at the point where the shiny hydraulic piston enters the cylinder. At the first sign of any such leak, get the cylinder overhauled. Don't attempt this repair yourself unless you have years of mechanical-repair experience. The valving, internal seals, and precision surfaces inside any hydraulic system need the

Figure 8-16. *Typical hydraulic fluid fill cap for the trim and tilt system. This one is on a midsize Mercury engine.*

care of a trained person as well as a good assortment of rather expensive special tools.

Here's a list of possible symptoms that could indicate a hydraulic problem with your system:

- Engine will not trim up or down. (Electrical system checks out okay.)
- Engine trims up, but not down. (Electrical system checks out okay.)
- Engine trims down, will not trim up. (Electrical system checks out okay.)
- Engine will not return completely to down position or returns part way with a jerky motion.
- Engine jerks when shifted.
- Engine begins to trim up when backing off throttle from high speed.
- Engine will not hold set trim position, or will slowly drop from tilted position after sitting for an extended period.
- Engine will not hold trimmed position in reverse.

Electrical Troubleshooting. As for the electrical side of this system, you should be able to troubleshoot and pinpoint any problems that may crop up. To begin with, you'll need the wiring diagram for your engine. Consult your workshop manual. Your multimeter will be the only tool you need to trace the circuit and find any faulty components.

Incidentally, if your problems seem to be related to the trim-limiting switch, which is designed to control the total arc of the engine's tilt, or the dash-mounted trim-indicator gauge and its sender, you'll need special tools only a dealer will have. These components are sold as accessories for many engines but are not available on others. Turn to your manual for advice, and check with your engine dealer for specific information about your particular system.

As far as normal electrical troubleshooting goes, we'll begin, as usual, with the simple things. Check the fuse for a start. Fuses can be hard to find in some cases as they are usually mounted in-line and look like plug connectors. Your wiring diagram will help you here.

Look for broken or corroded wires related to the circuit. Repair or replace any faulty wires or connectors.

Make sure your battery connections and the battery itself are in good condition. If everything looks okay, you will now need to trace the circuit.

Figure 8-17 shows the components of a typical electric/hydraulic trim system. This will give you a general idea of how to trace the circuit, but remember that this is a generic representation, and you should follow your workshop manual for the tests on your particular engine.

If your search leads you to a faulty electric motor (power gets to the motor's feed wires, but the motor doesn't operate), then the motor will have to be replaced. This is a fairly common problem, especially if rust and corrosion have attacked the case and water has entered.

Unfortunately, in most cases you won't be able to reach all the screws holding this motor to the hydraulic manifold unit without removing the engine from the transom of the boat. And then the motor needs to be

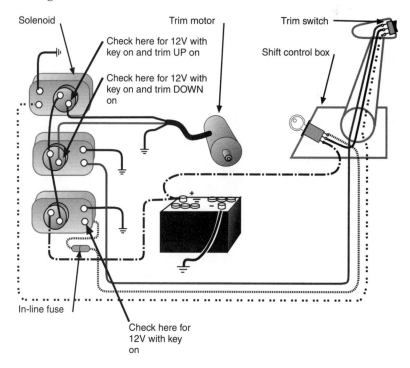

Figure 8-17. *Voltage-check points for a trim and tilt circuit.*

in the full "up" position, with the trailer lock engaged, to lift the motor off the manifold.

Replacement is simple enough if you can get to all the mounting screws, but be forewarned: This may not be as easy as it looks at first glance. If you don't have access to the proper lifting equipment, don't even attempt this task. Go to your dealer.

If you do have access to a hoist, lifting the engine away from the transom will expose the one or two screws, and allow easy removal. To accomplish this, though, you'll first have to remove the through-transom mounting bolts. There should be enough slack in fuel lines, shift and throttle cables, and steering linkage, to move the engine several inches away from the back of the boat, but once again, if you're in any doubt, you may want to reconsider your decision to tackle this task yourself.

Once the engine is away from the transom, remove the screws holding the motor in place and lift the motor

up off its seat on the hydraulic manifold. You will notice that the motor is sealed to the manifold with one, and possibly two, O-ring seals. These should be replaced when the new motor is installed. Failure to do so could allow seawater into the manifold, causing expensive damage. Once the motor is in place, rebolt the engine to the transom, and be sure to put some Life-Calk or similar sealer on the bolts before pushing them through the transom and bracket. Also, be careful to reroute the power feed and ground wire for the new motor through the installed grommets and through the holes cast into the engine bracket that lead up to the solenoid and relays mounted on the powerhead of the engine.

Again, let me advise caution. Improper routing of this harness could cause it to get pinched by the engine bracket as the engine tilts up and down, ruining the watertight harness built into the motor.

Chapter 9

The Cooling System, Lower Unit, and Propeller

For maximum efficiency, an engine should run as hot as possible without damaging itself. The simple fact is that the hotter an engine runs, the more power it generates from each stroke. Thermally efficient engines also are more economical and have cleaner exhausts.

But the process of internal combustion generates an excess of heat, and, left to their own devices, outboard engines would overheat and destroy themselves. So the cooling system has the job of keeping the engine's running temperature at the most efficient level, from the initial cold start right up to full-speed operation over extended periods.

Over the years, several methods have been used to cool outboard engines. We'll take a close look at the most common ones.

Air Cooling

Air cooling is a marvel of simplicity. There's little to go wrong, and few service requirements. Only the very smallest engines have used this method, though, and they're becoming quite scarce. None of the major outboard engine manufacturers uses this method of cooling today.

The last air-cooled outboard engine sold in the U.S. was a brand called Cruise-'n-Carry. These engines were made in Japan and distributed until the early 1990s through several major marine retail chains.

The advantage of these engines is their extreme lightness, compared to their water-cooled counterparts. The disadvantage is that they are extremely noisy. No quiet solitude as you motor along in your small boat with an air-cooled engine.

The reason for this is quite simple. The "jacket" on a water-cooled engine insulates the sound of the engine. The air-cooled design actually acts as a resonator and, if anything, amplifies the normal engine sound by way of the cast-in cooling fins that radiate heat away from the engine's combustion chamber.

Figure 9-1 gives the layout of a typical air-cooled engine, showing the fan, which is an integral part of the flywheel, and the cooling fins cast into the cylinder and the cylinder head. The flow of air over these fins is directed by metal shields and, in many cases, by the fuel tank bolted to the side of the engine block. Outer cases of plastic or stamped steel also help to guide cooling air over the engine and through the fins. As long as the engine is running, the flywheel/fan assembly is spinning, drawing air in through the top of the outer engine casing and forcing it downward over the fins and outward at the bottom of the powerhead.

About the only thing that can go wrong with this system is dirt blocking the fins. Dirt is naturally

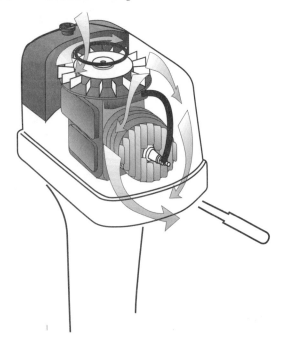

Figure 9-1. *Air flow in a typical air-cooled engine.*

attracted, of course, to any oily build-up on the fins caused by leakage or spillage from the fuel tank. It effectively insulates the fins and prevents them from doing their job of cooling.

Leaving a deflector shield or cover off the engine will alter the designed air flow over the fins, causing the engine to overheat. Fins broken through the engine's being dropped, or general carelessness, can also create hot spots in the cooling-air jacket.

Maintenance to the air-cooling system is easy. Periodically check to make sure all fins are clean and intact. Also, be sure all air deflector plates and covers are properly installed. That's it! There's nothing else required to service this system.

Air-and-Water Cooling. A second cooling system widely used on small engines employs a combination of air cooling for the powerhead and a water pump to keep the exhaust system cool. Service for this kind of engine will mean following the above-described procedure periodically, and also checking the water pump on occasion. Water pump servicing is described later in this chapter.

Water Cooling

Water cooling is the most popular method in use on outboard engines today. A "raw-water" pump delivers seawater to the engine powerhead, circulating it through the cylinder head(s), the bypass valve (also called a pressure-relief valve) or the thermostat, the exhaust housing, and back down through the engine midsection. The water runs down the exhaust cavity and away, either through an exhaust tube mounted aft of the propeller or—on the larger engines—through the propeller hub. In addition, water will also be exhausted through an exhaust-relief port that functions when the engine is in neutral and at idle. Figure 9-2 shows the water flow through a typical outboard engine.

Routine maintenance for your engine's water-cooling system is quite important, as severe damage can occur if it overheats. This is such an important system, that many of the latest engines incorporate overheat alarm systems, as well as speed limiters, in case the engine's operating temperature exceeds design limits.

Poor operating habits can play havoc with the cooling system. For instance, running the engine with the water pickup out of water can destroy the water pump impeller in a matter of seconds. Running in shallow water, kicking up sand and drawing it through the pump, can not only damage the pump itself, but send

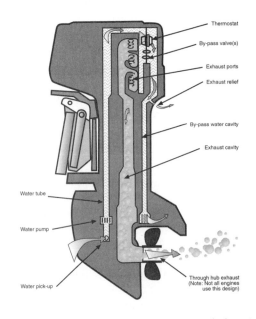

Figure 9-2. *Water flow through a water-cooled engine.*

debris up through the system, causing restrictions to the water flow through the powerhead and often creating localized overheating.

Symptoms of Overheating.
So what are the symptoms of overheating, and how do you isolate problems? Here are the classic symptoms:

- A "pinging" noise coming from the engine (detonation).
- Loss of power.
- A burning smell coming from the engine.
- Paint discoloration on the powerhead in the area of the spark plugs and cylinder heads.

If any of these symptoms appear on your engine, you should immediately seek out the cause and correct the problem. If the engine has overheated to the point where paint has discolored or begun to peel away from the engine, it's too late. Bring the engine to the shop and get it evaluated by a professional. It probably has damaged head gaskets, and perhaps even distorted cylinder heads and cases.

Causes of Overheating.
Here's a list of possible causes for engine overheating—not necessarily in order of probability:

- Fuel system problems, causing lean mixture.
- Incorrect oil-mixture ratio in fuel.
- Spark plugs of incorrect heat range. (Too hot.)
- Improper engine installation. (Too high on the transom.)
- Misalignment of engines in a dual-engine set-up.
- Faulty thermostat.
- Leaking or restricted water tube from pump to powerhead.
- Restricted water inlet.
- Faulty water pump impeller.
- Sand or silt build-up inside powerhead cooling passages.

If you have followed a routine maintenance schedule as described in Chapter 3, and think back again to the guidelines for troubleshooting in Chapter 4, you should be able to recreate this list in probable order. Here are the questions you need to ask yourself:

- Has the engine been run with the lower unit out of the water? If the answer is yes, suspect a burned-out water pump impeller.

- Have you serviced the water pump in the last several years as recommended by your engine manufacturer? If not, the pump could be simply worn out.
- Or, if the engine has many hours on it, the water tube from the pump to the powerhead could be restricted or even perforated.
- Have you done your daily visual checks? Has the pickup screen in the lower unit become restricted with sea growth or other debris?
- Did the overheating begin immediately after the spark plugs were changed? If so, suspect plugs of the wrong heat range. Check the number, and match it to the recommendation in your owner's manual or workshop manual.
- Are you certain the oil mix in the fuel is correct? Did the hot running begin just after a fill-up?
- Is the engine spitting, sputtering, or running rough? This could indicate a lean fuel mixture in one or more cylinders.
- Has the engine been run in shallow water, or run up on the beach, possibly drawing sand or silt into the pump, plugging the cooling system?

Once you have eliminated all of the simple and obvious things on this list such as a plugged water pickup, an incorrect fuel/oil mixture, or wrong spark plugs, the other checks will require partial disassembly of your engine.

Thermostat Removal and Testing.
If your engine is pumping water, as evidenced by the spray from the engine's cooling-system tracer nozzle, and all of the simple things have been eliminated, but the engine is still running hot, the problem may be a sticking thermostat.

Find out from your workshop manual where the thermostat cover is located. It's usually on the very top or side of the engine near the uppermost area of the cylinder head(s). If yours is a "V" engine, it will have one thermostat for each bank of the "V."

Remove the cap screws holding the cover in place. Lift the cover off the engine, and the thermostat and bypass valve will be exposed. With a pair of pliers, lightly grip the thermostat and pull it from the cavity it is plugged into. Often, you won't even need pliers— you can grasp the thermostat with your fingers and remove it.

Inspect the cavity and the thermostat for any build-up of silt, sand, seaweed, or other debris. If you find debris in the cavity, you'll need to flush the system, as explained later.

To clean the thermostat, use a medium-bristle brush and some warm, soapy water. Scrub off any build-up. Once it's clean, you can check the thermostat's opening temperature with simple kitchen tools.

To test the thermostat, fill a medium-sized saucepan with fresh water to about $1\frac{1}{2}$ inches (35 mm) below the rim. Place it on your kitchen stove.

Next, thread a section of small-diameter coathanger wire through the top of the thermostat as shown in Figure 9-3.

Bend the wire to allow the thermostat to hang from the edge of the pan, freely suspended in the water and fully submerged. Check your manual for the temperature at which the thermostat should open, and begin heating the water. Use a standard meat thermometer to monitor the water temperature.

Keep the probe of the thermometer no more than about $\frac{1}{2}$ inch (13 mm) from the thermostat for an accurate reading of the temperature the thermostat is exposed to. Carefully observe the thermostat as the water heats up.

The center of the thermostat should begin to open at the prescribed temperature, and open fully in short order. If not, you'll need to buy a new thermostat and install it.

If it does open at the correct time, you'll be certain that your hot-running problems are not caused by the thermostat, and your search must continue.

Whenever you reinstall a thermostat or a bypass valve, always use new sealing gaskets or O-rings for the cover. Any leakage here will splash cooling water all over your ignition system and cause corrosion.

Flushing Your Cooling System.
As explained in Chapter 3, periodic flushing of the cooling system is important, especially if you run your engine in salt water.

When you use a freshwater flush adapter, never turn the water pressure on full. Open the controlling spigot valve no more than about one-quarter of its maximum. Full water pressure from freshwater mains is far greater than the norm for any outboard system, and can damage internal seals in the cooling system.

Next, start the engine and run it to about 2,000 rpm in neutral. Run the engine long enough to bring it to full operating temperature, to ensure that the thermostat opens and fresh water circulates through the cooling system. This entire procedure should take between five and ten minutes.

This freshwater flush, performed on a regular basis, will go a long way toward ensuring that your engine's cooling passages stay clean and unrestricted for many years.

I have only one caution for you here, but it's very important: Never run your engine out of the water with the propeller installed. If the engine should accidentally be knocked into gear, you have the potential for a very serious accident.

Servicing the Water Pump.
No matter how careful you are, sooner or later you will have to remove your engine's lower unit and service your water pump. Removing the lower unit is not particularly difficult, but you must be careful to follow any special recommendations for your specific engine. This is another job that needs the aid of your workshop manual, at

Figure 9-3. *Testing a thermostat on the stove top.*

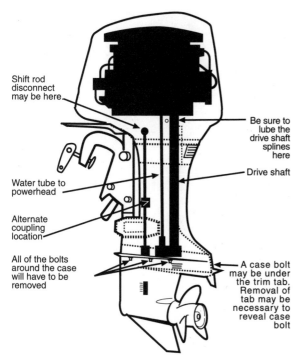

Shift rod
disconnect
may be here

Be sure to
lube the
drive shaft
splines
here

Drive shaft

Water tube to
powerhead

Alternate
coupling
location

All of the bolts
around the case
will have to be
removed

A case bolt
may be under
the trim tab.
Removal of
tab may be
necessary to
reveal case
bolt

Figure 9-4. *Disconnect points for removing the lower unit.*

great way to hold the assembly in place. Just be sure to shim the vise with some soft wood between the jaws and the skeg on your engine, so you don't mar the skeg.

To disassemble the water pump, begin by removing the O-ring seal at the base of the splines on your engine driveshaft, if your engine has one there. Next, remove the fasteners holding the water pump housing in place. Lift the pump housing up off its seat on the lower unit and over the end of the driveshaft.

Depending on tolerances, your pump impeller may slide out of the pump housing and have to be removed separately, or it may lift right out over the driveshaft inside the pump housing. It really doesn't matter which way it comes off, as you will ultimately want to remove it for inspection anyhow. Before you do anything, though, make a note of which way the impeller blades are bent in the housing. You may need to bend a new impeller's blades the same way.

Figure 9-5 shows the pump housing, rubber impeller, positioning key, and the lower end of the driveshaft as it enters the lower unit gearcase.

Once you have the water pump disassembled, carefully inspect the impeller for cracks in the rubber or wear to the tips of the blades. Bend each blade over and look for signs of cracking. Also, the impeller will have a plastic or bronze center hub that is vulcanized to the rubber. Make sure there is no separation evident here. This is a common point for the impeller to fail—the hub will spin as the engine driveshaft rotates, but the rubber blades will sit stationary, pumping no water.

Even if you see no cracks, or breakdown is not evident in the vulcanization between the hub and blades, the impeller should be replaced if the rubber feels stiff and the blades have taken a "set"—that is, if they remain folded over when you remove them from the housing. It's a sign that they'll give out soon.

In addition to the impeller, have a good look at the inside of the housing the impeller rotates in, as well as the stainless-steel base plate the impeller rides against. These often get grooved and scored if sand passes through the pump. If they are scored, they must be replaced along with the impeller. In this instance, I recommended you to get a water pump kit from your dealer. It will not only have a new impeller and housing, but also a full set of seals and gaskets for the pump and water tube. This is always the best way to go, but if you are trying to save a few dollars, it's possible to

least until you have been through the entire procedure. Once you've found all the fasteners, and followed any special instructions, such as whether the engine should be in forward gear, or how the shift linkage is disconnected, you should have no trouble with this job.

Figure 9-4 shows the fasteners you'll have to loosen to remove the lower unit. A special caution here, however. On some engines, particularly Johnson and Evinrude models, the shift-rod height is a critical adjustment. It is adjusted by threading the rod in or out at the point where it enters the lower gear housing. If you are careful not to turn this rod while you're servicing the water pump, no adjustment will be necessary.

But if you've turned the rod, or if you're in doubt as to its adjustment, get the height specification for your engine from your service manual and measure the distance as described in the manual.

Once you've removed the lower unit from the engine, you'll need to find a way to hold it upright while you work on it. If you have a workshop vise, this is a

Figure 9-5. *Typical pump housing, impeller, and impeller locking key.*

buy the impeller separately and use some brush-on gasket sealer to revitalize the old seals and O-rings.

When reassembling, use some gasket sealer, or thick grease, to hold the impeller key in place as you lower the impeller down the driveshaft and into place. Manufacturer's recommendations vary on the next step, but you should lightly coat the inside of the pump body with two-cycle oil—or the recommended proprietary grease called for in your manual to prevent the impeller blades from sticking to the inside of the pump housing during storage and initial start-up. As you lower the pump housing over the impeller, tuck the blades in place slightly as you turn the housing in a counterclockwise direction until all the blades are oriented correctly and inside the housing. Align the housing and push it all the way to its seat. Figure 9-6 shows this procedure being performed.

Once the housing is in place, coat the threads on the cap screws that secure the housing with some gasket-sealing compound and reinstall them. Be careful not to overtighten these screws—snug is the word here,

not as tight as you can get them. If you have a torque wrench, and know how to use it, a specification will be given in your manual, usually in inch-pounds, NOT foot-pounds.

With the pump in place and secured, you need to clean the splines on the engine end of the driveshaft, and lube it with the recommended grease. A high-pressure resistant, waterproof grease such as Moly-lube works well. Be sure to reinstall the O-ring seal at the base of these splines if your engine had one or requires one. Failure to reinstall this sealing ring could allow water to get in contact with the splines, causing the driveshaft to rust and seize inside the end of your engine's crankshaft. If this happens, you'll never be able to remove your lower unit again without causing extensive, expensive damage.

Next, inspect the copper water tube that connects the water pump to your engine's powerhead water jacket. Look for any signs of perforation in the side of the tube, and be sure it's not excessively bent or kinked. If either of these two conditions exists, the tube

Figure 9-6. *Pre-bending the new water pump impeller blades.*

will need replacement. This is quite unusual, but check it to be certain anyway. Note that the tube will often be slightly bent for alignment purposes; this is not cause for replacement. If you bought a complete kit for your water pump, new sealing rings will be included for the water tube. Be sure to use them.

Reinstalling the Lower Unit.
When you reinstall the lower unit to the engine assembly, there are several potential troublespots to watch. In the first place, be quite certain that the water tube engages with the hole in the water pump housing, and that the seal for the tube does not become dislodged when you try to push the lower unit up into the engine midsection housing.

Secondly, be sure to position the shift linkage properly, so that it goes up through the bottom pan of the powerhead and aligns correctly with the shift-lever linkage. Also, the drive shaft may have turned slightly when you were working on the water pump, and the

splines may need to be realigned slightly as you try to engage the driveshaft in the powerhead.

These three problems will make you wish you had three hands to line everything up and push the unit into place. That's the answer. Get a helper for this task.

With the cowl cover removed, disable the ignition system as I've described earlier. You may find it necessary to move the flywheel ever so slightly as you push up on the lower unit trying to engage it. Have the second set of hands move the flywheel for you, as you push up.

As for the water tube, the trick is to get everything into position, leaving just enough room to look up into the engine mid-section with a flashlight. With a thin screwdriver, move the tube into alignment with the hole in the top of the water pump housing, so that the final upward push will force the tube into the pump. Most of these assemblies have a tapered entry so that even if the tube is slightly out of alignment, it will self-align in the last 3/8 inch (10 mm).

As for the shift rod, depending upon the design, you may have to have your second set of hands align the water tube with one hand and the shift rod with the other. Once everything is set, the lower unit should slide up into position with relative ease. No hammering or pounding is recommended here. If it won't slide into place, something is misaligned. Drop the unit and check again to be sure everything is in its proper place. Don't force this assembly together. Keep your patience, and don't expect it to go together the first time. Seasoned professionals often make two or three attempts before getting everything lined up.

Once the lower unit is up in place, you'll have to reinstall the fastening screws for the gearcase. Before installing these bolts, however, coat the threads with some gasket-sealing compound. For a detailed explanation regarding this recommendation, be sure to read Chapter 10 covering corrosion problems and solutions.

When you've got the lower unit bolted in place, reinstall the steering trim tab, and if yours is the adjustable type, make sure to install it in the same position it was in when you removed it.

Last, hook-up your shift linkage in accordance with your workshop manual, and remember it's not recommended that you try to shift gears unless the prop shaft is turning, so don't force the shifter to test your work—you may damage the shift mechanism.

Now you can test your work by using your flush adapter and running the engine to see that it pumps water; or reinstall the propeller, put the boat in the water, and test it at the dock.

Testing the Overheat Alarm

If your engine is equipped with an engine-overheat alarm, it should be tested periodically. Most manufacturers recommend testing this system seasonally. Some engine models have a horn-test button built into the system, so checking is as simple as pushing a button every now and then. Other systems go through a self-test when the key is first turned on, until the engine starts.

It's important to note that these systems are designed not only to warn of overheating, but also of problems with the automatic oil-blend systems found on midsize and large two-stroke outboard engines. Check your owner's manual to determine which system you have, and be sure you know how to tell the difference between overheating and an oil problem. Mercury, for example, uses a steady horn beep to indicate overheating and an intermittent beep to indicate a problem with the oiling system.

Four-stroke engines will have a sensor screwed into the oil gallery of the engine, and a warning system for low oil pressure, as well as an overheating sensor.

Testing your overheating sensor is relatively easy. Use your workshop manual to help locate the sensor. On "V" engines, the system will usually have one sensor for each engine bank. The sensors are generally located on or near the cylinder head(s).

Be sure to identify the correct temperature sensors, using the color coding in your workshop manual. Many new engines have a special sensor that's activated at about 135°F (57°C) lower than the overheating sensor. This special sensor is used to initiate an ignition timing change as the engine warms up.

Once you have located the correct sensor, disconnect the one wire lead going to it and remove it from the engine. Next, fill a medium saucepan to within an inch of the top with your favorite cooking oil, and set it on a stove.

Set your multimeter to the low-ohms scale and attach one of the test leads to the wire on the sensor and the other to the metal body of the switch that fits into the cylinder head. Suspend the switch and test leads in the oil.

Get a meat thermometer and begin heating the oil with the thermometer probe set in the oil. Check the specifications in your engine service manual for the activation temperature. It should be somewhere between 230°F and 250°F (110°C and 121°C). Be certain to check the right temperature for your specific engine, however.

Now watch the thermometer and the ohmmeter. The latter should read infinity—indicating an open circuit—until the appropriate temperature is reached, and then it should give a reading of zero or near zero, indicating a closed circuit. Any deviation from these readings means the switch is bad and must be replaced.

Incidentally, the reason for using cooking oil for this test is simply that the boiling point of water is too low. Note also, there is no correlation between the temperature at which the switch activates and the actual temperature of an operating engine. The switch senses an average of the cooling-water and cylinder-head temperatures—and the cylinder head is usually much hotter than the overall coolant temperature.

To test the remainder of the overheating-warning circuit, that is, the wiring from the sensor, the horn itself, and the ignition power feed to the circuit, simply turn the key switch to the "on" position and ground the lead going to the temperature sensor to the engine block. The horn should sound.

If not, use the wiring diagram in your service manual and check for voltage getting to the horn from the ignition switch with the ignition key in the "on" position. If you can't find voltage going into the horn, then the problem is in the wiring or the connections from the ignition-key switch to the horn itself. If voltage is getting to the horn, but it will not sound off, try running a wire jumper lead from the ground connection on the horn to a known good ground near the horn, or the battery negative terminal if it is close enough. With the key turned on, and this jumper connected to the horn, it should sound. If not, the horn is faulty and must be replaced.

If the horn does sound when the jumper is attached to a good ground, then the problem with this circuit is in the wire coming from the horn to the engine-mounted sensor, and it will need repair or replacement.

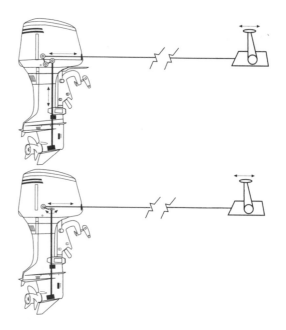

Figure 9-7. *The remote shift system, from control unit to propeller.*

The Shifting System

If your boat is equipped with an outboard engine with tiller controls, the shifting system is rather simple. It consists either of a lever mounted on the side of the powerhead or, on newer engines, a twist control that is combined with the throttle and part of the tiller handle. From either of these two points, the shift linkage connects to a shift rod that extends from the powerhead, down through the engine's mid-section, and into the lower unit gearcase itself.

Short of a catastrophic failure of the gear mechanism in the lower unit, this shifting system is generally quite trouble-free. Catastrophic failures are caused by neglect or misuse.

If your boat is equipped with remote controls, you will have a lever mechanism and a cable running from the remote to the shift linkage under your engine cowl in addition to the above-mentioned components. In either case, the shift mechanism begins at the actuation lever and ends at the propeller on your engine. Figure 9-7 shows a typical remote-control shift assembly, cable, under-cowl linkage, shift rod, and a shift-rod coupler entering the lower gearcase, in a typical arrangement.

Diagnosing Shifting Problems. Shifting problems fall into one of seven categories as follows:

1. Shift lever is hard to move.
2. Shift lever won't move at all.
3. Lever moves but no gear is engaged.
4. Won't come out of gear.
5. Shifts into wrong gear.
6. Goes into gear, but makes a loud "clunk" as it engages. (Not to be confused with the normal "clunk" of the dog clutch engaging during a normal rapid shift.)
7. Excessive noise from the gearcase.

Depending on your experience and confidence level, some of the possible causes for these symptoms may be best handled by your dealer, but at least you can approach the dealer with a good understanding of what is going on after you've read through this section.

Pinpointing the source of your trouble is a matter of using a process of elimination with shift systems, and the process for each symptom follows.

1. Shift lever is hard to move. You need to determine if the problem is in the control box or at the engine to begin with. To determine this, carefully disconnect the shift and throttle control cables at the powerhead. Be sure to observe the position of any positioning clips, and be extremely careful not to change the position of any adjustment nuts at the cable ends.

Now try shifting the lever at the remote control unit. Does it move freely now? Can you see the inner portion of the control cable for both the gear shift and throttle moving in and out as you work the shift lever? If the answer is yes, then your troubles are at the engine and not the control box.

If the shift lever action seems unchanged, then the problem is in either the control box or in the cable assemblies. Cable replacement necessitates disassembly of the control box unit, and it's recommended that you let the dealer handle this chore. The risk of making a mistake is too great, and improper cable adjustment can be a serious safety hazard. If your control and cable assembly is five or more years old, suspect either a seized cable or possibly a control-box mechanism problem.

If you determined that disconnecting the cables at the engine made the shifting seem normal, the next most probable cause for this trouble is the pivot point under the engine powerhead that connects to the shift rod going down through your engine's midsection.

Often there is a grease fitting for this pivot point, and it's frequently neglected as it's often difficult to get at. Inspect this area of the linkage, and if signs of rust are evident near the bushings that support this lever, you have located your problem. Lubricate, and try again.

If this lever is actually seized, it may be necessary to disconnect your shift rod in accordance with your service manual so that you can work the shift lever back and forth while you pump in new lubricant to the lever's pivot bushing. This lever must move freely to ensure smooth shifting. If the shift pivot lever on the engine doesn't appear to be seized, another common problem is a seized or hard-to-move pivot shaft on the shift lever. The pivot point should be lubricated periodically with products such as Mercury's "Corrosion Free" or OMC's "6-In-One" lubricant—especially if the control on your boat is left totally exposed to the elements all summer.

Once again, let me remind you not to try to shift gears unless your engine's running. Trying to force your engine into either forward or reverse when it's not running can damage the shift linkage and possibly the gear mechanism in the lower unit.

If you discover that the shift-rod actuation lever under your powerhead is working freely, and the problem is not at the control handle, then the problem is in the lower gear case. Check the gear-oil level in the lower unit, and be certain the correct fluid is installed in accordance with the manufacturer's recommendations. Unless it's just a matter of topping up or changing the lower-unit gear oil, correcting this problem will definitely require your dealer's services.

2. Shift lever won't move at all. Follow the exact procedure outlined above for hard movement. Usually, if the lever is seized completely, the problem is in the control box. But, if the problem occurs during commissioning after an extended lay-up of the boat, a seized shift cable is probable.

3. Lever moves but no gear is engaged. This is generally a cable problem. What has probably happened is that the clamp fixture that holds the outer sheath of the shift cable in place under the engine cowl has broken or somehow become detached. Visually check at that point, and if no movement of the outer sheath is evident, check at the point where the cable exits the back of the control box. If the cable is moving here, the problem is inside the control box and it will have to be opened up for further inspection. Any movement of the outer sheath while the shift lever is moving can create this problem.

If the shift cable is properly secured at both ends, and the shift will not engage any gear, check to be certain the shift rod is attached at the pivot point under the powerhead—see Figure 9-4. If this connection appears to be okay, you'll need to check your service manual to determine if the shift linkage has a coupling for the shift rod inside the engine's midsection, as many of the Johnson/Evinrude engines do. If you have this type of shift rod connection, and are running an older engine, the midsection may have a small access plate that can be unscrewed. Simply remove the plate and check the two screws that hold the shift-rod connecting clamp in place. On newer and extended-shaft engines, this plate has been eliminated, and the lower gearcase will have to be unbolted and lowered several inches to reveal this shift coupling. In either case, if the coupling or the upper pivot-point attachment bolt is loose or missing, you will have found your problem. If the cable control and these connections are okay, then the only remaining cause for your shift problems is inside the gearcase.

4. Won't come out of gear. Follow the same diagnostic sequence as for Number 3 above.

5. Shifts into wrong gear. Check cable outer sheath attachments at the engine and control box as already described.

6. Makes a loud "clunk" when either forward or reverse is engaged. Check to be sure the engine itself is secure to the transom of the boat. If it's not, correct as required. If the mounting bolts are tight, check the lower steering pivot point on the engine. These generally have a rubber-shock mount located inside the attachment housing that connects the steering point to the engine midsection. After many years of use, these mounts can break, causing the engine to jerk when you shift into gear, creating a metallic "clunk" as it does.

Incidentally, failure of these mounts can also cause the steering to seem loose. To check the mounts, simply grab the lower unit and try to move it backward and forward. Look for any excess movement between the mount bracket and the engine's midsection. If movement is evident, the mounts will have to be replaced.

If the engine mounting checks out okay, the clunking noises you hear when shifting must be coming from only one place—inside the lower gearcase. Gear damage has occurred. To verify this, drain the lower unit gear oil and look for metal particles in the oil. Also, check the magnetic drain plug for any chunks of bearings or gears. If they're evident, you've pinpointed your problem.

7. Excessive, strange noise coming from the lower gearcase. Check the fluid level in the gearcase. It's also possible that a seal has leaked, allowing the gearbox to fill with water. If the oil is milky, then water has entered the unit and it will have to be removed for resealing by the dealer. If the fluid is simply low, you may be lucky and able to stop the noise by adding oil.

Generally, however, once a noise is generated it means that a bearing or gear has been run without adequate lubrication long enough to cause damage. If the noise continues after adding fresh oil, you've waited too long. A gear-unit overhaul is indicated.

Lower-Unit Maintenance

Some routine maintenance for the lower unit is covered in Chapter 3. Essentially, you need to change the gear oil seasonally, being careful to check for water in the oil—look for milky discoloration—and to keep a close daily look-out for any signs of oil leakage or fishing-line build-up at the forward edge of the propeller.

The procedure for changing the oil is described in Chapter 3. In addition, you will want to remove and inspect the propeller seasonally and lubricate the propeller shaft. Figure 9-8 shows a propeller being removed for annual inspection.

Here's something else you can easily do to save the lower unit from a major breakdown: Check the propeller shaft for excessive run-out (bending) while you have the propeller off. A bent propeller shaft will not always show up as excessive vibration as you might expect, and the run-out can cause the propeller shaft seals to fail prematurely, causing oil to leak out of the unit or water to leak into the gearcase.

If this happens, you will not only need a new propeller shaft, but gears and bearings as well—a considerable expense. One grounding of the propeller can bend the shaft beyond allowable limits, especially if your boat is equipped with a stainless steel propeller. The blades on these props are strong, and will resist

Figure 9-8. *Propeller being removed for inspection.*

bending and chipping, bending the shaft before the propeller itself shows much sign of damage.

To check for a bent shaft, you'll need to make a "jig" out of an old coat hanger. Bend the coat hanger so that the tip of the wire comes as close as possible to the edge of the very end of the propeller shaft.

Figure 9-9 shows the coat hanger properly in place. Use duct tape to hold the jig in place securely on the lower unit. Make sure the engine is in neutral, and disable the ignition as described in previous chapters of this book.

Now slowly turn the prop shaft through 360 degrees. If the clearance between the end of the coat hanger and the edge of the shaft changes even the slightest amount, the shaft is probably bent. Manufacturers allow anywhere from about 0.004 inch (0.102 mm) to a maximum of 0.010 inch (0.254 mm)—not very much.

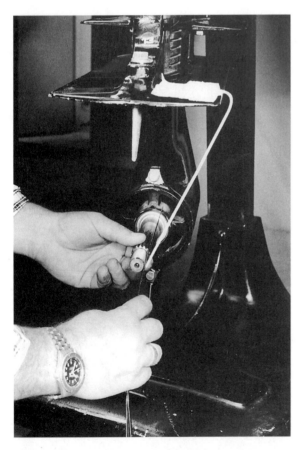

Figure 9-9. *Checking for propeller-shaft run-out.*

If your check shows any variation in distance from the end of the coat hanger wire to the edge of the shaft, you can determine the exact amount of bend by turning the shaft to the point where the maximum clearance is visible and sliding feeler gauges between the coat hanger and the shaft until a slight drag is felt. The thickness of the feeler gauge indicates the amount of shaft run-out. Match this number to the specifications for your engine as found in the workshop manual. If the bend is excessive, the propeller shaft will have to be replaced as soon as possible to avoid further damage.

Beyond normal inspection of the lower unit, oil changes, and seasonal greasing of any fittings located in your shift linkage at the engine, it's also a good idea periodically to lightly lube the shift cable where it exits the outer sheath and attaches to the shift lever under the engine cowl. (Do the same for the throttle cable.) Use some white lithium grease, available at marine and automotive supply stores. Also, inspect the throttle and shift cables for their entire length from the remote-control unit back to the engine, and look for any signs that the outer sheathing is chafed or cracked. If you detect damage, you should immediately wrap the affected area with electrical tape to help seal the outer case and prevent water intrusion into the inner cable. Keep in mind that if the outer sheathing has been chafed through, water has already migrated into the cable and caused damage. The tape is only to prevent further water migration into the cable. Get the cable replaced ASAP. Don't take this lightly; it can be a serious safety hazard. How would you like to end up flying across a lake with the throttle cable stuck wide-open?

Choosing a Propeller

For long engine life and best overall performance you need exactly the right propeller. But no single propeller is right all the time. If you change the way you use your boat and motor, you may have to change the propeller, too. The wrong propeller will not only affect performance, but can destroy your engine in short order.

If you bought your engine and boat as a combined package, your dealer will have matched the propeller as part of the pre-delivery rigging procedure. Be sure to verify this with the dealer, and if in doubt, perform the test outlined at the end of this chapter. But things may change while you own the boat. The dealer will have selected a propeller based on the average load for your boat. But you may be adding heavy items that will alter this important criterion for propeller selection.

Outboard-powered houseboats and pontoon boats are prime examples of craft liable to accumulate heavy gear. Perhaps you've just started to tow water-skiers. Perhaps you originally used your engine as auxiliary propulsion for a small sailboat, and are now using it as the primary propulsion for a lightweight skiff. Or maybe you've taken to visiting mountain lakes. Extreme changes in altitude can affect the engine's operating range. If your engine was propped for sea level, operation on a high-altitude lake may require a different propeller to keep the engine revving within its normal range. In fact, all these changes will require re-propping.

The goal of the engine rigger is to ensure that your engine reaches a specified number of revolutions per minute (rpm) at full throttle under the normal circumstances of use for your boat. No more, no less. Typically, this top engine speed falls into a range with a tolerance of 800 to 1,000 rpm. The range is always listed in the workshop manual for your engine, and is generally listed in the owner's manual as well.

Before continuing with any explanation of propeller theory, let's define some basic propeller terms.

Propeller Terms

Pitch. This specification states the theoretical distance in inches that the propeller moves forward or backward in one complete revolution. Think of the propeller as a screw, turning its way into the water.

Diameter. This is the straight-line distance from the center point of the hub to the most distant tip of any of the propeller's blades, times two.

Cupping. This term describes the "curl" at the trailing edge of a propeller blade. Cupping is used by engineers to increase the blade's theoretical pitch, giving it a better grip on the water.

Slip. This is related to pitch. The theoretical distance a propeller will move through the water in one revolution (pitch) is affected by the fact that the propeller will actually lose some distance due to slippage through the water. Typically, a standard propeller will have anywhere from 10 percent to 30 percent slip, depending upon its design and use.

Blade thickness. The design of the propeller and the material used determine the thickness of the blades.

Ideally, blades are designed as thin as possible to reduce drag. But they also need thickness for strength.

Cavitation. There are many causes of cavitation, including excess loads on the propeller that create vapor bubbles on the blade surface. The effect is to make the propeller lose its grip on the water and revolve at excessive speeds. Cavitation can be caused by some underwater disturbance in front of the propeller, something as simple as a barnacle on your engine's lower gearcase, or a depth-sounder transducer mounted near the centerline of the boat. Nicks on the leading edge of the propeller blades can also cause this condition. Cavitation can cause extreme damage to the propeller blades, deep pitting, and ultimately, loss of the blade itself.

Ventilation. This is a condition similar to cavitation, but usually involves air drawn down from the surface. Sometimes this comes about through too much "out" trim of the engine, or having the engine mounted too high on the transom. Sometimes exhaust gases are drawn into the area of the blades. Your lower unit has a ventilation plate to prevent air from being sucked down into the propeller from the surface.

Rake. This is the aft-leaning angle between the propeller hub and the blade. High rake angles are used on performance boats to overcome an increased tendency toward ventilation and cavitation.

In addition to the basic definitions, you'll need to know several other key facts to work your way through the basic propeller selection process.

The method used by manufacturers for basic propeller identification (in addition to the model number of the prop) is to give first the diameter and then the pitch of the prop in inches. They're usually stamped on the propeller hub. For example, a prop stamped "14 × 17" has a diameter of 14 inches and a pitch of 17 inches. Any additional markings will be special to the manufacturer, identifying the propeller model and general type.

As for the specific type of propeller to use for your application, you will need to get a copy of your engine maker's accessories catalog (available free at all dealers) and look at the propeller-recommendation list. It's set up for specific horsepower and type of use, as well as boat weight or type. Simply find your boat's category, (pontoon boat, ski boat, runabout, etc.) and the horsepower for your engine, and you will be close to finding the right prop for your boat.

To determine the exact diameter and pitch that's best for you, study the specification chart more closely. Diameter, for example, will be determined by the approximate normal speed for your boat, and generally the manufacturer will list several possibilities based on this specification.

To determine the exactly correct pitch, you will need to do some testing on the water. I must point out that the only way to perform this test accurately is with a tachometer. If your boat doesn't have one, you will have to let the dealer set this up for you with his shop instrument.

Here's the test sequence:

1. Consult your owner's manual to establish the specified range of revolutions per minute (rpm) your engine is designed to reach at full throttle. This is sometimes referred to as wide-open throttle, or WOT.
2. Using your existing propeller, establish a "benchmark" by making several test runs in fairly calm water. Adjust your engine's trim angle to achieve maximum speed. Record your maximum engine rpm, and the speed achieved if you have a speedometer.
3. If the full-throttle rpm exceeds the recommended range, you need more pitch. Install the manufacturer's next-larger-pitch propeller and retest. On average, changing the propeller pitch by one inch will change engine speed by approximately 250 rpm. That is, engine speed will increase by 250 rpm if you decrease the pitch one inch, and decrease by 250 rpm if you increase the pitch by one inch.
4. If the full throttle rpm is below the recommended tolerance, install the next-lower-pitch propeller available and retest.

You will have achieved the optimum adjustment when you can just get the maximum rpm specified for your engine with the boat loaded as it normally would be. This should also give you the best speed.

For installations on non-planing craft, such as heavy workboats and auxiliary sailboats, rpm is the most critical of the specifications in this evaluation process. If the boat is not reaching hull speed, too coarse a pitch may be preventing your motor from developing its maximum rpm, and therefore full horsepower.

Chapter 10

Dealing with Corrosion

The manufacturers of outboard engines have spent many hours researching and experimenting with metal alloys, paint, primer, and metal-coating systems to minimize the corrosive effects of the marine environment. In the last several years, manufacturers of large outboard engines have even come out with special models, such as the "Saltwater Series" from Yamaha and the "Ocean Pro" series from OMC. These engines use more stainless steel components to answer the concerns this market has had for premature rusting and corrosion of exposed metal parts and fasteners on the engines.

Even with all the improvements in metal and paint technology in the last five or six years, corrosion and rust are still concerns for the outboard engine owner. Nevertheless, with a little care and maintenance, you can keep your engine looking like new for years.

Sacrificial Zincs

Unless it's very small, your outboard engine will have at least one sacrificial zinc "anode" mounted on it in the area that rides below the waterline.

Webster describes an anode as "the positive terminal of an electrical source." Now you are probably saying, "Wait, I never knew my outboard engine was an electrical source." Well it is—when it's submerged in water, and most especially in salt water. The unprotected aluminum alloys used in your engine's casing

and block assembly are quite vulnerable to what is known as galvanic corrosion.

Any metal submerged in salt water is subject to the corrosive effects caused by the water. Essentially, the salt water acts as an electrolyte, allowing the passage of an electric current. Add different metals to the electrolyte, and you have created a primitive electric cell, busily transferring metal from one terminal to the other.

Metals fall into two categories, anodic or cathodic, depending upon their atomic makeup. Further, alloys are made of more than one type of metal, offering a blend of dissimilar metals to the saltwater electrolyte in one solid piece—your outboard engine. These dissimilar metals will begin to react when exposed to an electrolyte, with each metal having its own potential voltage, or the ability to produce a small electric charge.

Anodes are the most reactive of the underwater metals used. They're often described as the least "noble," referring to the galvanic series of metals.

The Galvanic Series

Anodic or Least Noble (Most Active) End of the Series

Magnesium and its alloys
CB 75 Aluminum alloy (used for anodes)
Zinc
B 605 Aluminum alloy (used for anodes)
Galvanized steel or iron

Aluminum (various alloys used in boatbuilding)

Cadmium

Mild steel

Cast iron

Lead/tin solder (50/50)

18-8 Stainless steel, type 304 (active)

Lead

Tin

Manganese bronze

Naval brass (60 percent copper, 39 percent zinc)

Nickel (active)

Yellow brass (65 percent copper, 35 percent zinc)

Red brass (85 percent copper, 15 percent zinc)

Copper

Silicon bronze (various alloys)

Nickel (passive)

18-8 Stainless steel, type 304 (passive)

Titanium

Platinum

Cathodic or Most Noble (Passive) End of the Series

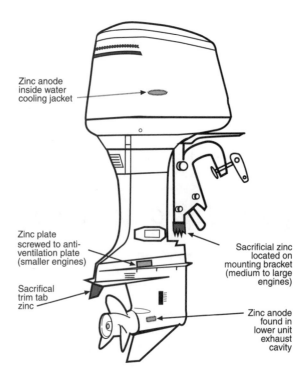

Figure 10-1. *Typical anode locations.*

The idea is to try to neutralize the voltage potential between underwater metals in order to minimize electrical current flow, and to protect the anodic characteristics of the casting your outboard engine is made of. The "cathodic" metals such as lead, titanium, bronze alloys, and certain stainless steel alloys are much less affected by galvanic corrosion, and with the exception of titanium, due to its scarcity and extreme cost, are often used in underwater hardware and fittings.

The simplest way to achieve protection for underwater metals is to provide a sacrificial piece of metal and let it gradually get eaten away by this underwater electrical activity. This means using a metal that falls near the top of the galvanic series, above the metals it is protecting.

Two metals are widely used today. The first is a zinc alloy and the second, more common on new engines, a very pure aluminum alloy that is far more anodic than the casing on your engine.

One of the first steps in protecting your engine is to be sure all the zinc anodes are installed correctly, and in good condition. Figure 10-1 shows the typical locations for these anodes on the exterior of the engine and mounting bracket of larger engines.

These zincs are available from your dealer. Many aftermarket manufacturers also produce replacements

for popular engines. They're available at marine supply stores.

Checking zincs is just a matter of seeing if they are eroding away. Zincs that are eroded to about two-thirds their original size should be replaced. Also, it is important to remember that they should be checked periodically as outlined in the maintenance intervals described in Chapter 3 of this book.

For any engine that is left in the water, either at a mooring or in a slip, a frequent look to see how rapidly these anodes are dissolving is quite important. Many factors contribute to the longevity of your engine's zincs. Stray, leaking current from shore-power cords, electrical problems from a boat nearby, salinity, water current, and whether the water is dirty or clean—all form part of the equation. Just because your buddy says his zincs last two seasons doesn't mean yours will last three weeks. (If yours really last only three weeks, however, there definitely is a serious underwater electrical problem near your boat.)

Besides a visual check, zinc anodes can also be checked using your multimeter. These anodes must be electrically "bonded" to your engine if they are going to work. Zincs that are attached over freshly painted surfaces, or have been painted over themselves, will not do their job. The paint will act as an electrical insulator, negating the zinc's electrical potential.

To test for electrical continuity between the zinc and your engine case, begin by setting the ohmmeter scale on your multimeter to read low ohms. Next, take a pocket knife and scrape away a shiny clean spot on the zinc to use as a point of contact for the red test lead from your meter. Next touch the black lead from your meter to a known engine ground (such as the one for the ignition module/powerpack). You should get a low ohm reading on the meter, near zero.

If your meter gives no reading, then there is a break in the electrical flow between the zinc and the body of your engine. To correct this problem, you should remove the screws holding the zinc in place and thoroughly clean the surface under the mounting point. Make sure the threads for the mounting screws are clean, shiny metal. If necessary, scrape away excess paint to provide a good, shiny metal surface for the zinc to mount on, and reinstall the zinc. Check your work by performing the ohmmeter test again and looking for a low ohm reading on the meter. Any zinc that has inadvertently been painted over should be replaced with a new one. Figure 10-2 shows the zinc continuity test being performed with an ohmmeter.

On some engines, the manufacturers have gone a step further and provided additional zinc protection inside the engine's cooling-water jacket. Access to these zincs requires removal of the engine cylinder head(s) and should be done by your dealer. Normally, on engines that are tilted up when at a mooring or in a slip, most of the corrosive water drains out of the engine, so replacement of these zincs is an infrequent matter. You should find out if your engine is equipped with these internal anodes however, and establish the replacement frequency. Remember that many manufacturers recommend periodic removal of the cylinder head to get rid of excess carbon inside the combustion chambers. If your engine's equipped with internal zincs, that would be the ideal time to replace them.

In addition to the zincs themselves, many large engines use small, uninsulated stainless-wire links to connect the lower section of the engine to the powerhead section electrically, ensuring a good electrical bond. Frequently, though, these links break, creating a

Figure 10-2. *Using an ohmmeter to test continuity between a zinc and the engine case.*

weak point in the corrosion-protection system. Inspect the wires at least annually to make certain they are still connected and in good condition.

Touching Up Paint Chips and Corrosion

Sooner or later, your shiny new engine will begin to show its age. Paint will begin to chip off the lower unit, and rust will begin to show on the steel parts still widely used by all makers for things like tilt mechanisms, trim-motor housings, steering arms, and many of the bolts and fasteners that hold your engine together.

Not only is this corrosion and rust unsightly, but it can also create some miserable disassembly problems when the need arises. Proper cleaning, priming, and touching-up of these corroded surfaces should be a part of every outboard owner's annual maintenance routine.

Figure 10-3 shows an example of neglect, resulting in paint bubbling and blistering in many spots on the lower unit. What has happened to this particular engine is that the paint has been chipped and left unattended for several years. The corrosive effects of salt water have worked their way up and under the paint and begun to eat away at the metal underneath. As this chemical reaction occurs, the paint begins to lift and eventually will fall off the engine.

To halt this corrosive action you must remove all traces of loose, flaking paint and corrosion, and thoroughly clean and prepare the surface for a special primer coat of paint and the final color coats.

Begin by using a single-edged razor-blade scraper, and scrape all the loose paint and corrosion away. Next, get some medium-grit sandpaper and sand away any remaining traces of corrosion. Be sure to overlap your sanding efforts onto the good paint that surrounds the blistered section by about 1/2 inch (13 mm).

Next, use a solvent such as acetone to wipe down the sanded area and remove dust and traces of oil from the surface.

Figure 10-4 shows the surface sanded and ready for inspection. If the corrosion has pitted the metal surface, you will want to fill the pits with an epoxy-based putty such as Marine-Tex or Plastic Aluminum. For a quality repair, you will want to bring the metal "up to surface."

To fill low spots on the surface, mix the epoxy and catalyst according to the product instructions. Next, take a body-putty applicator and spread the epoxy putty onto the prepared surface as shown in Figure 10-5.

Curing time for the putty will vary according to ambient temperature and the product itself, so again, follow the manufacturer's instructions. Once the putty has fully cured, sand the area again with medium-grit paper until all excess putty is removed and only the pits in the metal are filled with the epoxy. Wipe down the area again with solvent. You are now ready to spray a coat of surface primer on the area.

Unlike autobody repair, your outboard engine will require a special primer that is formulated to provide extreme corrosion resistance to aluminum and magnesium parts. Standard automotive or steel primer

Figure 10-3. *Neglected engine, showing advanced corrosion of the lower unit.*

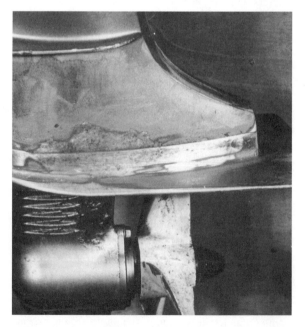

Figure 10-4. *Corroded area sanded and ready for inspection.*

Figure 10-5. *Filling corrosion pockets with epoxy putty.*

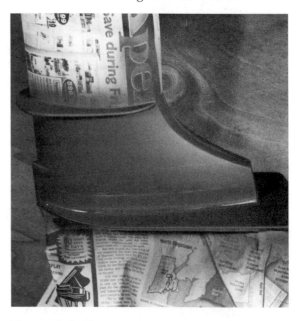

Figure 10-6. *The corroded area masked off and ready to spray.*

paints won't do the job here. Currently the only approved primer for aluminum is based on zinc oxide. It is available at any marine store dealing with outboard engines or inboard-outboard drives. A popular brand is made by Tempo Products. This primer is yellow in color.

Before spraying the primer over the repaired surface, you'll want to mask off the engine to avoid getting yellow overspray on the areas not requiring fresh paint.

Figure 10-6 shows the area masked, with about 2 inches (50 mm) of overlap where the primer and a color coat can be blended into the surrounding surface.

Before painting, you should make certain the area is well ventilated. Wear a respirator and safety glasses. Hold the spray nozzle about 12 inches (300 mm) away from the surface and apply a light coating of the primer onto the area to be covered, keeping the spray nozzle in motion. Try hard not to let the paint build up as you spray close to the masking tape. Any build-up here will leave a distinctive ridge when the tape is removed. The idea is to gradually thin out all coats of paint as you overlap onto the area just beyond the edge of the actual repair. You will need two or three coats of the primer to ensure adequate coverage and protection.

Allow about 15 minutes between coats. After the final primer coat has been applied, allow an hour or two for the paint to cure.

Next, lightly sand the primer with fine-grit sandpaper, making sure to sand out any runs in the paint, and focusing on the primer that overlapped onto the painted area beyond the edge of the actual repair. Now you are ready for the color coats.

As with the primer, paint colors are available at dealers and marine supply houses to match your specific engine make and model year, duplicating your engine's color as it left the factory. The problem here is that the paint on your engine has been out in the sun, and exposed to the elements for several years, and the paint will not be a perfect match. Typically, engine paint will fade as it is exposed to the sun, and the touch-up will be slightly darker in color.

This may mean masking off a larger area and spraying a section of the engine to avoid a blotchy, spot-touched look after the repair is made. This will be up to the individual, and the specific area being touched up. As with the primer, you will more than likely need at least two coats of color paint, and possibly three, before the yellow primer is fully coated and invisible.

After the color has been applied, allow plenty of time for all layers of fresh paint to fully harden, generally overnight. Remove all the masking tape and paper. Next, take some regular automotive-grade rubbing compound and rub out any excess overspray around the perimeter of the repair, to blend the edge in with the surrounding paint. Once a smooth, well-matched surface is achieved, wax the area with a good grade of automotive wax to complete the repair.

Figure 10-7 shows the completed touch-up on the same blistered spot shown in Figure 10-3. Minor chips in the paint, such as often occur on the skeg section of the lower unit, can be repaired with a light hand-sanding, solvent wash, and application of zinc-oxide primer and a color-matching touch-up with a small artist's brush.

Dealing with Hardware Corrosion

It's not only chipped paint, and the consequent corrosion of aluminum, that you have to worry about. Your engine also has parts that are made of steel and painted over. These will eventually begin to rust, and if you have a light-colored engine, such as the white Johnsons and light-colored Yamahas and Mariners, this rust

Figure 10-7. *The corroded area completely refinished.*

will be quite unsightly. It's also damaging if left unattended.

A really great product is available to help eliminate this problem. It's called "Rust Reformer" and is marketed in the U.S. by Rust-Oleum. This thin gray liquid is simply painted on over a prepared rusted surface and allowed to cure overnight.

To prepare the surface, simply scrape away any loose rust and solvent-wash the metal to remove any accumulated oil film. Thorough sanding is not needed as the reformer dissolves the remaining rust, leaving a black "skin" over the surface. If desired, the black coating left by the cured reformer can be painted over with a color-matching paint.

Figure 10-8 shows this product being applied to a rusted tilt tube on an outboard engine. This product can be used on rusted bolt heads before paint touch-up, with great results, just be sure to give it plenty of time to cure before applying the color coat—typically overnight.

Releasing Fasteners and Preventing Corrosion. At some point, you may have to remove a bolt that is frozen into the aluminum casting on your engine. This is an especially common problem with the bolts that hold your lower gearcase to the midsection of the engine. These bolts always have to be removed to service your water pump, so keeping their threads from seizing can save you many hours of frustration and grief.

Prevention is the best policy here. Even though these bolts are generally made of stainless steel, they are threaded directly into the aluminum casting of your engine's midsection, and after a few years of use, especially in salt water, will try to become one with the case.

A good preventive measure is to remove these bolts as shown in Figure 10-9 and brush on a non-hardening gasket sealer such as Permatex #2, available at any auto parts store. Coat the entire bolt and thread it back into the engine. This coating will minimize water penetration and seal the threads against its corrosive effects.

In the field, you may hear people who recommend coating these same bolts with white lithium grease or Lubriplate. Although this grease has many uses around a boat, it is not recommended for underwater applications. This grease is not waterproof, and will eventu-

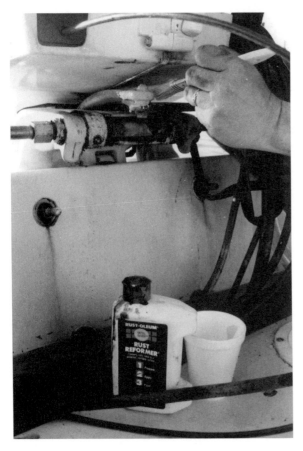

Figure 10-8. *Applying "Rust Reformer" to part of the outboard engine.*

Figure 10-9. *Coating a bolt from the lower unit with gasket sealer to prevent corrosion.*

ally dry out, leaving behind a non-protective, chalky powder. Another uninformed recommendation may be to use a product generically described as "anti-seize" for underwater applications. Anti-seize is made with microscopic metal particles, usually copper. Spreading this all over your stainless bolts and then screwing them into a casting made of an aluminum/magnesium alloy simply adds another dissimilar metal to the corrosion/electrolysis equation. These products should not be used on an outboard engine's underwater parts.

Frozen Bolts. If you work on your own engine long enough, sooner or later you will encounter a bolt that simply refuses to budge when you try to remove it. The trick in dealing with this problem is to know when to quit trying.

Don't break the bolt off inside the engine. That will surely require the services of an experienced mechanic to get the remains out of the casting without causing further damage. Penetrating oils and miracle "rust buster" products usually do not work on aluminum, and are generally a waste of time, so don't place much trust in this method. But if you are careful, you can usually apply some heat to the area around the bolt and get it to loosen up.

Before applying heat to a casting on your engine, pause for some safety considerations. You will be using an open flame from a propane-fired torch just like the ones plumbers use to solder pipes together. Most do-it-yourselfers have one of these in their tool collection, so even if you don't, you will find it easy to borrow one.

Begin by being certain all fuel and fuel tanks are

removed from the area. You will need to be careful not to melt any wire insulation or plastic parts in the immediate area of the bolt you are trying to remove. Also, remember that on small pieces, the propane torch can heat the metal to the point where it will actually melt and ruin the casting. So be careful, and apply only enough heat to loosen the bolt and no more.

Lastly, you need to know up-front that to get the piece hot enough for the bolt to loosen, you will burn the paint on the engine in that area and it will have to be retouched.

The technique for using heat to loosen a bolt is simple, but most people do it wrong. The idea here is to expand the metal around the bolt and its threads, allowing just enough clearance to unscrew the bolt.

Do not heat the bolt itself. This will expand the bolt in the hole, making it even tighter. Heat the area around the bolt, keeping the torch in motion at all times. Keep applying pressure to the head of the bolt as you heat up the casting, until it begins to turn. At this point, back the bolt out and remove the heat.

Figure 10-10 shows the correct procedure for heating and removing a frozen bolt. Notice the concentration of the flame, not on the bolt but on the case, and the wrench on the bolt head applying pressure.

After everything cools down, you can clean the

bolt with a wire brush. To clean the hole and threads in the casting, use some "Rust Buster" or WD-40. Spray some penetrant into the hole and work a clean bolt of the correct size and thread pitch in and out of the hole until it works freely. Then, you can blow out the displaced corrosion by using some of the carburetor and choke spray described in Chapter 7 with an extension nozzle. Just be careful not to get any of this spray in your eyes (wear safety glasses), or on a painted surface, as it will damage the paint. Once completely cleaned, you can reassemble the components, using light oil on bolts above the waterline, or the gasket sealer already described on bolts below the waterline.

Saving a Drowned Engine

In almost 30 years of boating, I have seen five outboard engines go overboard. One of them was in water more than 100 feet deep, and to my knowledge it's still on the bottom. The other four were recovered and saved, and two of those are still in service.

The point is, losing your engine overboard is not the end of the world, but you will have to act quickly if this ever does happen. Also, some of the necessary procedures will have to be performed by your dealer to

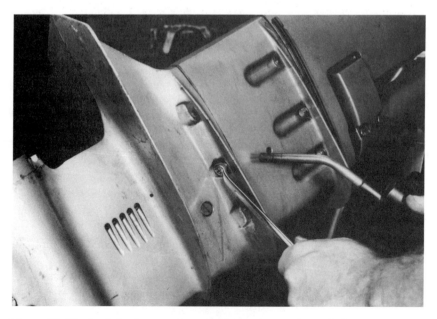

Figure 10-10. *Applying heat and pressure to remove a frozen bolt.*

ensure a total recovery and long life of the affected parts.

If your engine cannot be serviced within three or four hours after recovery, it should be submerged in fresh water until a complete recovery procedure can be performed. Once the engine is exposed to air, the corrosive action of the water in and on the engine will begin, so you need to minimize this exposure.

The first step is to disable the ignition by disconnecting the plug that connects your ignition power pack to the charge coil under the flywheel. Next, remove the spark plugs and lay the engine in a position so that the spark-plug holes are facing downward. Next, spin the engine over by turning the flywheel by hand. You will see water pumping out of the spark-plug holes.

Once all the water is drained from the cylinders, mount the engine in a vertical position and disconnect the fuel lines. If you can reach it, there may be a drain screw in the float bowl of your engine's carburetor. Remove the screws and drain the water from all the carburetors.

Next, spray some outboard engine two-stroke oil into the spark-plug holes to coat the cylinder walls. This will take care of the emergency first aid part of the recovery. The next step will require the assistance of your dealer.

All of the electrical equipment on your engine will have to be removed, thoroughly rinsed in fresh water, dried and sprayed with WD-40 or a similar product to displace any remaining water, and then dried again and reinstalled. Note: Depending on the design of the electrical coils under your flywheel, your dealer may recommend replacement instead of simply cleaning and lubricating them. Unless the coils are completely epoxy-sealed (and many aren't) water will have migrated into the metal laminates of the coil winding core, and rusting will have started already. As the rust progresses, it may actually expand the core and break the wire winding around it, causing premature failure of the charge, sensor, or lighting coil. Ask your dealer for his experience with engines of your type, and take his recommendation. This procedure will include the complete disassembly of electric starter motors, and disconnecting all electrical connector plugs for a thorough cleaning and drying. In addition, you or your dealer will have to remove and disassemble all carburetors on the engine and flush them out. Note that you can use the cleaning procedure described in Chapter 7 to take care of this.

It's important to note that in many cases, simply removing the water from the cylinders, draining the carburetors, and drying off the ignition system will get the engine to a point where it can probably be started and run. But neglecting the starter motor (if it has one) and the charge coils and sensor coils located under the flywheel will cause these components to fail prematurely, so don't leave them out of the cleaning procedure just because the engine is running.

Once the engine is ready to run, give it a double oil mix (the same mixture that you'd use for new engine break-in) for the first few hours of operation to completely coat internal parts and force out any remaining water.

Once the mechanical and electrical recovery steps have been completed, the exterior of the engine should be washed and waxed with a good grade of car wax to complete the procedure. If proper care has been taken in this revival process, you can rest assured your engine will live a normal life. But carelessness here will reduce your engine's life expectancy by many years. Don't cut corners with these procedures.

Chapter 11

A Look at the Future

As this book goes to press, the outboard-engine industry is entering a new age. Mandates created by the U.S. Environmental Protection Agency (EPA) have dictated that by the year 2006, all two-stroke outboard engines must reduce their hydrocarbon emission levels by 75 percent.

Such huge reductions have forced the engine makers to develop new technology that will not only reduce the emission levels and the characteristic smoke that all two-stroke outboards are known for, but as an additional bonus, will improve fuel economy by 30 to 40 percent. Further benefits include smoother running, easier starting, added power, and ultimately, increased reliability. Just as we have seen in the cars we drive, trouble-free operation with lengthened service intervals will be the norm as this new wave of engines evolves.

Some fear that this new generation of computer-controlled engines will make it impossible for do-it-yourselfers to perform any work on their own engines. But the truth is that not much is going to change for people who want to do some of their own maintenance. Such jobs as winterization, oil changes, spark-plug replacement, filter changes, zinc replacement, cooling-system service, and the routine touch-up of nicked paint will remain essentially unchanged.

An Era of Increased Reliability

While it's true that significant differences in these new engines will affect an owner's ability to service the fuel and ignition systems, the good news here is that as these systems evolve, the reliability level will be so high that the service requirements of these two vital systems will be reduced to changing filters and spark plugs. These are jobs you can easily undertake.

From a troubleshooting perspective, you should remember that the needs of an engine, as we've discussed in this book, are not going to change. The only difference here is that we will see injectors used to deliver fuel to the combustion chamber(s) of the engine. A series of sensors will tell a small computer how long to activate the injector(s), based on such things as altitude, temperature, and engine load. This same computer will automatically adjust ignition timing to provide the optimum setting under any working conditions.

This may all sound too good to be true, and skeptics will still say, "Yeah, but what do I do when these sensors break down, or the computer fails?" These people need to be reminded that outboards have used solid-state electronic ignition systems for 20 years, and although they're not totally trouble-free, they've proven themselves in the marketplace. Skeptics should also look at what has happened in the automotive industry over the last 20 years. Modern cars are far more reliable than their antique cousins. The equipment that outboard makers will be using has a long automotive history of reliability under extreme operating conditions. Tolerances and manufacturing techniques have been proven. These new engines are going to be a great improvement over what we have available to us now.

A Range of Choices

The race to produce an engine that meets the government requirements and satisfies the demands of customers has created several different designs, with each manufacturer claiming to have come up with the best answer. Only time will tell who has the best system. At the time of this writing, only a limited number of these engines have been produced, and they have only been in service a few months. It's interesting that all of the new two-stroke systems are based on fuel-injection systems.

Meanwhile, some manufacturers, such as Honda, have taken the position that the four-stroke engines they have been improving on for years are the answer. These engines are quiet, smooth-running and much easier to adapt to emissions requirements than a two-stroke unit. Yamaha, Johnson/Evinrude, and Mercury have expanded their four-stroke offerings on smaller engines, and Yamaha is planning to extend its four-stroke range to 200 hp by the year 2000.

Four-stroke engines may work well in many applications, but their problem is weight. The four-stroke simply cannot produce as much horsepower per pound as a two-stroke at this time. Larger boats with outboard engine power need the high horsepower edge that only a two-stroke can produce, assuming weight limitations.

The Mercury/Mariner DFI System

The first company to announce a new system was Mercury. Its system, known as "DFI" for Direct Fuel Injection, was created in a joint venture with an Australian company, the Orbital Engine Corporation, which has strong roots in the research and development of automotive fuel-injection systems. The development of the new DFI engine began in 1987 and the first offering is a 200-hp engine, available under either the Mercury or Mariner trade name.

This engine uses a modified version of Mercury's existing V6, 3.0-liter engine block. All other aspects of the engine, such as the midsection and gearcase, are essentially unchanged from the currently available engines. Cylinder heads and pistons have been significantly modified to accommodate the fuel-injection system.

With this system, a blend of pressurized air and fuel is injected into each cylinder via the fuel injector. This highly atomized blend of air and fuel is sprayed from the injector at the spark-plug end, offering greatly improved combustion efficiency. The timing of both the ignition and fuel injection spray are controlled by the system's on-board computer or electronic control unit (ECU). Improved atomization over carbureted designs, combined with precisely metered fuel volume, based on atmospheric as well as load conditions, are the secrets of this system's lower emissions and greater fuel economy.

In addition, unlike existing engines, fuel, air, and oil from the crankcase don't enter the combustion chamber until the exhaust ports are completely closed, so the mix burns completely. This also greatly reduces the volume of "raw" oil and unburned mixture entering the exhaust system and ultimately the atmosphere. If you refer back to Figure 1-4 on page 5, you'll see how present-day two-strokes allow these partially burned gases to escape from the combustion chamber. Figure 11-1 shows the DFI system layout.

A unique feature of the DFI system is the need for a pump to provide pressurized air for the injector to mix with the fuel, which is pressurized by a separate pump. The fuel, which is pressurized to 90 psi, and the air, which is pressurized to 80 psi, are carried via fuel/air "rails" to a direct injector. At the point of injection, the fuel and air are mixed as they enter the combustion chamber. This air pump, which is belt-driven, is not used by other systems. Periodic inspection and replacement of this belt will be an additional maintenance item for owners of these engines.

Another challenge for engineers working on the design of the DFI (as well as OMC's new system) was the need to provide for adequate lubrication of the crankshaft, connecting rods, piston undersides, and all the supporting bearings for these vital components. Two-stroke outboard engines have always been lubricated by the blend of fuel and oil drawn into the crankcase via the carburetor. With the DFI system, fuel is injected directly into the combustion chamber of each cylinder, never reaching the crankcase. So, an oil metering and distribution system was designed that sprays two-stroke oil into key areas of the crankcase. This system uses an electric pump controlled by the ECU. By controlling oil injection electronically, Mercury engineers have been able to reduce the amount

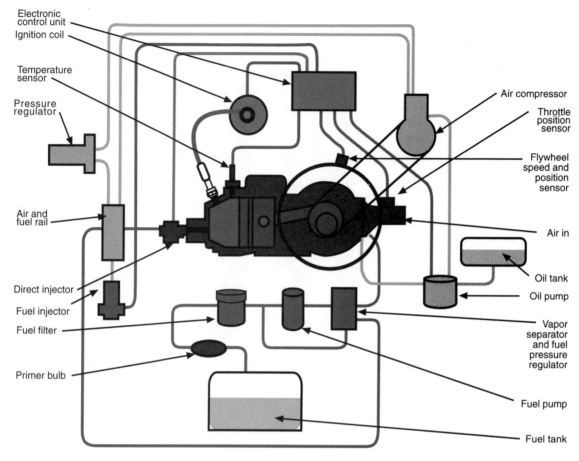

Electronic
control unit
Ignition coil
Temperature
sensor
Pressure
regulator
Air and
fuel rail
Direct injector
Fuel injector
Fuel filter
Primer bulb

Air compressor
Throttle
position
sensor
Flywheel
speed and
position
sensor
Air in
Oil tank
Oil pump
Vapor
separator
and fuel
pressure
regulator
Fuel pump
Fuel tank

Figure 11-1. *The Mercury/Mariner DFI two-stroke system.*

of oil needed for lubrication, greatly reducing oil burning, a classic fault with two-stroke engines. Two-stroke oil is stored in a remotely mounted tank, just as with present technology, but since the new engines use approximately 50 percent less oil, fill-ups will be less frequent.

Another important design feature of the DFI system is the use of a fuel/vapor separator that forms an integral part of the fuel-delivery system. In automotive fuel-injection applications, fuel is delivered to the injection system in bulk, and whatever fuel is not used at a given time is returned to the fuel tank through an additional fuel line. This constant circulation of fuel

from the tank to the engine and back not only provides a constant supply of fuel at the injectors, but also helps to cool the injectors as fresh fuel circulates through the system. This feature is undesirable in marine engines, however, because engineers seek to minimize the length of fuel line and number of connections in the system, thereby reducing the possibility of leaks, and in general, simplifying the system.

The fuel/vapor separator provides the needed circulation, but eliminates the need for a return fuel line routed all the way back to a remote tank. All circulation occurs between the fuel injector and the fuel/vapor separator with delivery back to the injector via the high-pressure fuel pump. This equipment is all built into the powerhead and is an integral part of the injection system.

The Johnson/Evinrude (OMC) Ficht System

During the 1980s, OMC also was searching for ways to improve two-stroke performance, emissions, and fuel economy, just as Mercury was. Initially, OMC, like Mercury, centered its efforts on the Orbital Engine Company's design. Prototypes were built and extensively tested. But, in OMC's opinion, the Orbital design had too many flaws. OMC engineers felt the Orbital design was too complex, and had problems with spark-plug fouling and a tendency to overheat pistons.

Then OMC discovered a design created by the Ficht Engineering Company in Germany. This design is simpler than the Orbital technology, but offers the same essential advantages as the Orbital design. OMC took a new tack, abandoning the Orbital technology. The result is their Ficht Direct Injection system, introduced on their 1997 150-hp model. This system produces an average of 35 percent better fuel economy, reduces emissions by 80 percent and, like the Mercury DFI system, uses an average of 50 percent less lubrication oil. As with the Mercury DFI system, this engine provides virtually smoke-free operation and is much smoother and quieter than existing engines.

Again like the DFI system, the Ficht injection system uses sensors and a computer (ECU) to process information about atmospheric pressure, temperature, and engine loads. Both systems use a high-pressure fuel pump and an ECU-controlled oil-injection system. Both have a fuel/vapor separator to provide for fuel circulation between the fuel injector and the high-pressure fuel pump. Both systems only inject fuel/air mix after the combustion chamber exhaust ports are fully closed.

The essential difference between the two systems is in the injectors themselves. With the Ficht system, there is no need for an air pump and extra lines to transport the air from the pump to the individual injectors. There is no belt to service and extra parts are eliminated. Air for mixing with the fuel is provided in a more conventional way, through an air intake in the crankcase, where it is pressurized by the downward stroke of the piston. As with existing engines, the air enters the combustion chamber via intake ports in the side of the cylinder.

Fuel is delivered by the injector directly into the combustion chamber, but at a much higher pressure than that of the Mercury/Orbital system. The Ficht fuel injector is essentially a piston-type pump that uses an electro-magnetically controlled valve to force the piston through a close-tolerance bore to "hammer" fuel through the tiny orifice at the tip of the injector nozzle. Because of the extremely close tolerances, this injector is able to inject the fuel into the combustion chamber at pressures of about 250 psi. This electro-mechanical marvel is so precisely made that it can repeat this piston-pumping cycle up to 100 times per second, based on the needs of the engine as computed by the ECU.

In terms of troubleshooting, the task is simply to determine if fuel is getting to a particular cylinder. If not, the need is to establish if the ECU is sending an electrical pulse to the injector. If it is, the injector must be replaced. Replacement is as simple as threading the unit out of the cylinder, much like a spark plug. Of course, if no cylinders are getting fuel, then the problem is in the fuel delivery system, and would be diagnosed similarly to an existing carbureted system.

Yamaha's Answer

While Mercury and OMC have been busy developing totally new engines, Yamaha decided to adapt existing automotive technology to the marine environment. The result is their new 3.1-liter electronic fuel-injection (EFI) two-stroke outboard, available in 225 hp and 250 hp configurations. Both use a special sensor to measure oxygen content in the engine's exhaust. This sensor will tell the ECU if the exhaust mixture is too rich or too lean, and the ECU will adjust fuel-delivery rates accordingly.

This system has another feature borrowed from existing car engines (as well as heavy diesel engines). At engine speeds of between 500 and 2,000 rpm, the ECU actually cuts out two of the six cylinders, turning the engine into a more efficient four-cylinder unit able to meet the power needs of the boater at slow speeds—when trolling, for example. During tests, this

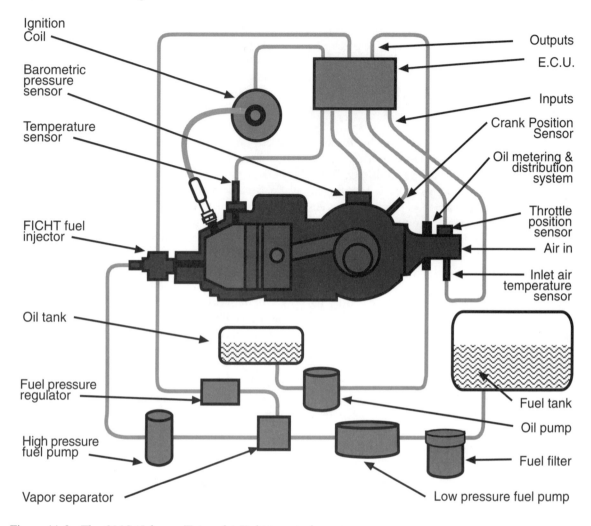

Figure 11-2. *The OMC (Johnson/Evinrude) Ficht two-stroke system.*

engine achieved a 36 percent improvement in fuel economy over its carbureted counterpart.

As with its DFI counterparts, the Yamaha system uses an injector for each cylinder. But rather than inject the fuel directly into each individual combustion chamber, the injector is tied into an individual "throttle valve" mounted in the same location as the old familiar carburetors.

Lubrication is accomplished by Yamaha's familiar "Precision Blend" oil-injection system, which injects a calibrated amount of oil just downstream of the throttle valves, just as the existing system does.

The advantage of this system over its competitors is that the price increase over the carbureted version is only about 5 percent—something most consumers can easily justify against a 36 percent decrease in fuel costs.

Looking ahead, Yamaha is presently testing a 200-hp two-stroke using a catalytic converter. Development of a catalytic converter for marine use is quite a challenge. Automotive converters run at extremely high temperatures, and trying to integrate this technology into the limited space available under an outboard engine cowl is no easy feat. Yamaha's answer was to create a water-cooled unit that will contain the heat within the unit but cool the exterior shell of the converter to approximately 180°F (82°C).

Looking Ahead

One thing is clear: In the future, the outboard engine will need sophisticated electronic systems to control its operation. Will this affect the ability of the Saturday-morning mechanic to perform some of his or her own routine service? No. As already stated, many of the maintenance items discussed in this book will be performed in exactly the same way as they are now.

While it's true that diagnosing running problems will require the services of a trained technician in many cases, the fact is these new engines will be so reliable that owners won't mind the occasional visit to a dealer. With proper maintenance as described in this book, the outboard engine will continue to provide many hours of trouble-free pleasure, compared with the few hours needed for servicing.

Index

ignition switch, 29, 30, 32
   testing, 39–41, 55–57
   tilt-type, 41
ignition system, 29, 30–43
   automatic advance in, 31
   capacitive discharge (CD) units, 31, 39
   capacitor in, 31
   CDI unit (module) in, 29, 30, 31, 38, 43, 56
   kill switch, 30, 32
   module testing, 38–39
   problem checklist for, 35
   spark tests, 33–34
   stop control for, 32, 39–41
   testers for, 30
   tests of, 32–41
   wiring for, 28
   See also under coils
ignition timing, 18, 22
   checking, 42–43
   optical, 43
   plate for, 31

J

Johnson products, 19, 23, 48, 58, 80, 101, 121, 123
jumper leads, 23

L

Life-Calk, 96
Loctite, 88
loran signal problems, 46
lower unit, 14, 105
   maintenance of, 107–08
   reinstalling, 103–04
   removing, 100–01
   See also under gearcase
Lubriplate, 116–17

M

maintenance, routine, 9–24
   daily checks, 9–10
   monthly checks, 10–11
   seasonal checks, 11–18
manuals, factory workshop, xi, 6
Marine-Tex, 114
Mariner products, 121, 122

Merc-O-Tronic products, 30
Mercury products, 7, 15, 23, 31, 35, 37, 41, 56, 82, 83, 93, 94, 106, 121, 122
metals, 110–11
metric hardware, 23
Moly-lube, 102
monthly maintenance checks, 10–11
muffs, 23, 24
multimeter (VOM), 23, 35–36, 45, 47, 52

N

noises. *See* sounds
Nylock self-locking prop nut, 12, 13

O

ohmmeter. *See* multimeter
oil, 1, 29
   changing, 2–3, 13–14, 18, 22, 84
   checking level of, 9, 21, 29
   excess, 84
   fogging, 16, 22, 24
   gearcase, 13–14
   grades of, 8
   incorrect, 29
   inspecting, 13, 20
   leaks of, 27
   level of, 29
   mix ratio, 8, 80, 99
   old, 29
   seals for, 9
   TCW-3, 8, 80
oil fill pumps, 14
oil filter, changing, 2–3, 19, 22, 84
oil injection systems, bleeding of, 83
   electronic, 121–22
   failure rate of, 28
   leaking, 27
   maintenance of, 17–18, 22
   mechanical oil-pump systems for, 82–84
   oil reservoir filter screen in, 81–82
   Precision Blend, 124
   ratchet clamps for, 81
   variable-ratio oiling (VRO), 80–82, 83
oil mixing. *See under* oil injection *and* oil
oil pump, 2, 84
oil recirculation systems, 84
oil sump, 2, 84

changing oil in, 18, 22
drain plug for, 2, 18–19
oiler. *See* oil injection systems
Orbital Engine Company, 121, 123
Outboard Motor Corporation (OMC) products, 7, 15, 31, 56, 80, 82, 84, 106, 111, 121
overheat alarm, testing, 104–05
overloaded boat, 2

P

paint, discoloration of, 26
primer, 114–15
safety when using, 115
touching up, 113–16
Permatex #2, 116
pinion gear, 60–61
piston, 1, 2, 3
seizure of, 57
piston rings, 3, 7, 15
Plastic Aluminum, 114
pollution, exhaust, 1
Precision Blend oil injection, 124
primer. *See under* carburetor
propeller, 25, 29
cavitation, 29, 109
choosing, 108–09
cupping of, 109
diameter of, 29, 109, 110
hub on, 11–12, 22
maintenance of, 9, 11–13, 21, 22, 107–08
pitch of, 29, 109, 110
rake of, 109
run-out, 107
safety, 100
slip of, 109
ventilation of, 109
propeller shaft, 11–13, 22
checking, 108
pump, oil, 2, 84
oil fill, 14
See also water pump
putty, 114

Q

Quicksilver DVA adapter, 23

R

radio, electrical noise in, 46
rectifier, 45
testing, 47–49
regulator, voltage. *See* voltage regulator
Ring Free, 8
rod, connecting, 1, 3
Rust Buster, 118
Rust Reformer, 117, 118
Rust-Oleum products, 116

S

safety, 11, 16, 25, 58, 64–65, 76, 100, 115, 118
screwdriver, using to detect sounds, 25–26
seals, oil, 9
seasonal maintenance, 11–18
SeaStar steering, 90
shift lever, 105–06
shift linkage, lubrication of, 10, 11, 21
shift rod, 2, 101
shifting system, troubleshooting, 105–07
sight, in troubleshooting, 26
6-in-One, 106
skeg, 2
smell, in troubleshooting, 27
smoke. *See under* exhaust
Snap-On Tools products, 33
solenoid, 51, 52, 56
sounds, in troubleshooting, 25
spark, 43
testing for, 33–34
spark plugs, 31–32
defective, 28, 29
gapping tool, 32
heat range of, 99
inspecting, 16
oil's effect on, 34
over-torquing, 34
replacing, 17, 22, 34
surface-gap type, 32
testing, 34–35
wires for, 28, 35–36
spark tester, 23
spring commissioning, 24
starter, manual, 57
pinion gear for, 60–61
pull cord replacement, 58–59
recoil spring replacement, 60–62
rope for, 57–58